# Beginner's Guide to iOS® 11 App Development Using Swift™ 4

## Xcode, Swift and App Design Fundamentals

### Serhan Yamacli

**Manchester Academic Publishers**

Publishers

D0830636

Beginner's Guide to iOS 11 App Development Using Swift 4 – First Edition

This book is dedicated to my parents...

# Table of Contents

# Chapter 1

## INTRODUCTION

Welcome to your guide to iOS® 11 app development.

This compact book aims to teach app development for iOS devices using Swift™ programming language. You don't need to have app development experience to learn the concepts and projects presented in this book. I'll assume that you have no knowledge on programming and app development. I'll try to explain every bit of app development process with plain words and will try to make things easy to understand. This book will take you as a beginner and at the end of the book; you'll be able to create your very own apps that are ready to run on actual devices and also ready to be sold at the App Store®. By the way, I'd like to remind you that a single book cannot make you an expert on a subject. However, this book will teach you a lot and you'll have a solid background to learn more afterwards.

As you might have heard, iOS apps have been developed using a programming language called Objective-C® for a long time. However, Apple recently introduced a new programming language: Swift. They announced Swift in the World Wide Developer Conference (WWDC) in 2014. In that year, first version of Swift was released. After some important modifications, Swift 2 and Swift 3 came around and finally Swift 4 is released in September 2017. Swift was a proprietary project in the beginning but now it is open source and a lot of developers contribute to this promising language. Swift has a more active community compared to Objective-C by September 2017 therefore your investment on learning Swift is a good choice.

As you follow this book, you'll go through the following steps:

**1.** Using Xcode® integrated development environment

**2.** Coding in Swift programming language

**3.** Designing user interfaces for your apps

**4.** Developing real world apps that will teach a lot in practice

**5.** Utilizing internal devices like GPS in your own apps

I'll not introduce complicated subjects until I'm sure that you understand the basics because it is very easy to get lost while learning a new programming language. You'll not be in such a situation with this book. I'll try to teach new concepts in the simplest way possible. Please don't forget that learning a programming language is a non-stop process, it never ends and this book will help you to get started easily.

Now, you know the aims and the method of this book. Let's set up Xcode 9 integrated development environment on our Mac®. By the way it is worth noting that the development environment we will use can only be installed on a Mac.

Chapter 2

# SETTING UP YOUR DEVELOPMENT ENVIRONMENT

In my opinion, one of the good things about Apple products is that their version number usually increases periodically making it easy to track. For example, the release years of iPhone® series follow this pattern: iPhone 5 in 2012, iPhone 5s in 2013, iPhone 6 in 2014, iPhone 6s in 2015, iPhone 7 in 2016 and iPhone 8 in 2017. Similar patterns are also observed in most of their software versions. In our case, Xcode versions are important.

## 2.1. Xcode Development Environment

**Xcode is an integrated development environment (IDE) for developing native software that runs on Apple devices.** It means that if you want to develop native apps for iOS devices, for Macs, for Apple TV® and for Apple Watch®, you do this using the software called Xcode. Xcode is developed by Apple and it is free to download and use. However, it is worth noting that Xcode can be installed and ran only on a Mac. Therefore, you need a Mac in order to install Xcode and start developing iOS apps.

Xcode has several versions each corresponding to the year it is released. For example, Xcode 7 was made available in 2015. Then, in 2016 Xcode 8 came and Xcode 9 is released in 2017. You may say "why are we so interested in this version thing?" It is because the appropriate version of Xcode is required to develop apps for specific iOS versions. Moreover, each Xcode version is bundled by different Swift versions.

## 2.2. Swift Programming Language

**Swift is a programming language that is used to develop apps for iOS®, Mac OS®, watchOS® and tvOS™** (and for Linux® recently). Xcode is bundled with Swift therefore you don't have to separately

11

download anything related to Swift. Swift has gone through important changes while evolving from the first version of Swift (Swift 1) to Swift 4. A code you have written in the Swift 1 or Swift 2 probably will not be valid in Swift 3 or Swift 4. This is called as "code incompatibility".

Xcode 9 has the updated Swift 4 language inside. Xcode 9 supports also Swift 3 however it is of course a good idea to develop in Swift 4 for continuity.

## 2.3. Installation of Xcode

**How to install Xcode?** Xcode 9 can be downloaded from the App Store on your Mac. Just go there and search for 'Xcode' (without quotes). It will show Xcode ready to be downloaded as shown in Figure 2.1 (All figures shown in this book can be viewed in colour and in full resolution on the book's website: www.yamaclis.com/ios11). Just click "Get" as shown inside the smallest rectangle in Figure 2.1 then it'll be downloaded and installed automatically in a while depending on your Internet connection speed (1 min~20 mins). As you can see from Figure 2.1, your Mac OS version should be at least 10.12.6 to install Xcode 9 (shown inside the rectangle at the bottom). Moreover, this download page shows that Xcode 9 includes Swift 4 and iOS 11 SDK (Software Development Kit) meaning that in Xcode 9, you can use Swift 4 to develop iOS 11 apps (shown inside the big rectangle). After successful installation, launch Xcode by clicking on its icon in the Launcher and then the welcome screen shown in Figure 2.2 should appear. As you can see from this figure, my Xcode's version is 9.0.

## 2.4. Setting up Signing Identities

In Xcode, you will develop iOS apps however, in order to build them (making the executable) for running on simulators or real iOS devices, **you need to sign the app**. Signing is a proof which shows that the app cannot be modified by anybody other than you hence assuring users that the app is from a trustable developer. Therefore, signing is essential and have to be done for every app you develop in Xcode. The good news is that once you set up code signing in Xcode, you can easily sign all your apps.

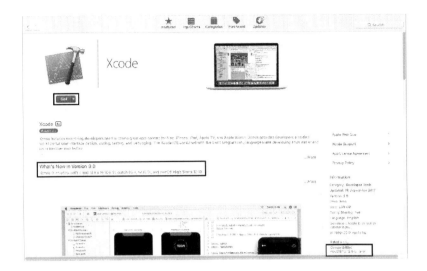

Figure 2.1. Xcode 9 download screen in the Mac App Store (colour images on the book's website: www.yamaclis.com/ios11)

Figure 2.2. Xcode welcome screen

If you want to develop apps in Xcode and try these apps on simulators or on your own devices, you just need a usual Apple ID for code signing. This process is free. However, if you want to sell/distribute your apps on the iOS App Store, you need to enrol in the Apple Developer Program which currently starts from $99 per year. Details of the Apple Developer

13

Program can be found on their official site: https://developer.apple.com/support/purchase-activation/. Since you're just beginning iOS development, you may continue without enrolling in developer program for now. You can always do it later when you are ready to sell your apps.

Setting up code signing is simple: just go to the Xcode menu as shown in Figure 2.3 and click on the "Preferences..." button.

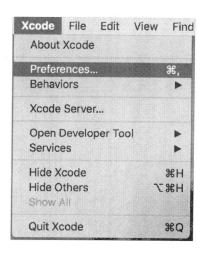

Figure 2.3. Xcode menu

When you click on the "Preferences..." button, you'll see a window as in Figure 2.4 which shows a very detailed set of preferences regarding Xcode's general settings. Click on the "Accounts" tab shown by the arrow. Then you'll see the window shown in Figure 2.5. Click on the plus sign (+) indicated by the lower arrow (1) and then click the "Continue" button shown by the upper arrow (3) while "Apple ID" is selected (2). After you enter your own Apple ID and password in this window, click the "Sign In" button as shown in Figure 2.6.

Figure 2.4. Preferences window of Xcode

After you add your Apple ID and password to Xcode, you'll see the window shown in Figure 2.7. In this window, click "Manage Certificates..." button as shown by the arrow.

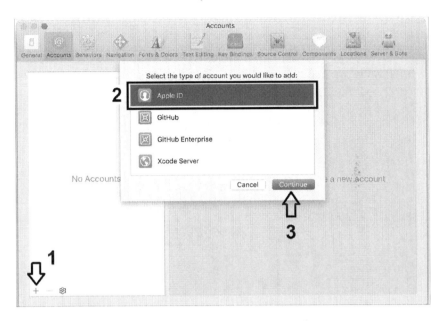

Figure 2.5. Adding a new Apple ID in the Accounts window

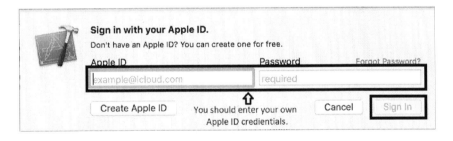

Figure 2.6. Adding your Apple ID to sign your apps

Click on the "+" button as shown by the arrow (1) in Figure 2.8. Then, select "iOS Development" (2). When you click "Done" button (3), your signing profile will be ready and shown as in (4). You can now close the "Accounts" window. If you did all these without a mistake, you did successfully set up your Xcode environment with the signing identity.

## 2.5. Viewing Installed Simulators and Devices

There is one step remaining to develop and test our first app. That is: setting up (or viewing) simulators in Xcode 9. Simulators are programs that mimic the behaviour of real devices. Therefore, you don't need to have all possible devices to test your app, you can use their simulators. The good news is that simulators of most devices are already installed by default when you install Xcode 9. To view the installed simulators, select Window → Devices and Simulators from the Xcode's main menu as in Figure 2.9.

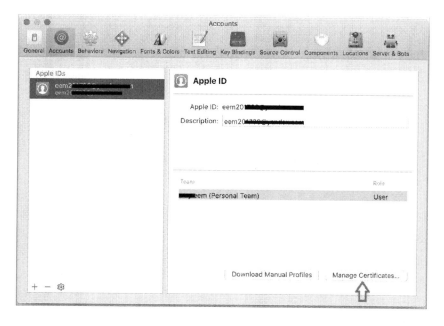

Figure 2.7. "Manage Certificates..." menu to add an app developer profile

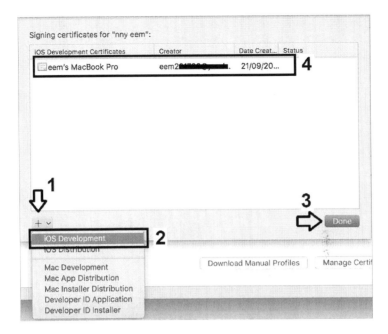

Figure 2.8. Creating signing profile for your Apple ID

Figure 2.9. Viewing device simulators already installed in Xcode

Xcode will show available devices and simulators in this window as in Figure 2.10. "Devices" tab shows the real hardware connected to your Mac. If there are no real devices connected to your Mac, the "Devices" tab will be empty as it can be seen from Figure 2.10. Click the "Simulators" tab to see the available simulators as in Figure 2.11. In Xcode 9, simulators of all up-to-date devices are already installed. The iOS versions and other information regarding these simulators are shown when we select the simulators from the left frame as in Figure 2.11. All simulators have iOS 11.0 by default.

After reviewing the installed simulators, we are now ready to develop our "Hello World" app in the next chapter.

Figure 2.10. "Devices" tab in the "Devices and Simulators" window

Figure 2.11. "Simulators" tab in the "Devices and Simulators" window

Chapter 3

# TEST DRIVE: THE HELLO WORLD APP

## 3.1. General Procedure for Developing an App

A good convention to start learning a programming language and a development environment is to try a "Hello World" example. It is just displaying the "Hello World" expression on the screen. OK, I know it is not an app that you'd be proud of showing to your family or friends but its usefulness stems from testing whether your programming environment is working properly and to see if you're ready to go for real projects. In our very first iOS 11 project, we will write "Hello, World!" in the middle of our device screen in any colour and font we like. We will test it on simulators but if you have access to an iOS device, you can test your "Hello World" app on it too.

Before we start building our first app, I'd like to point out general steps of app development:

**1.** Creating the Xcode project,

**2.** Setting up the User Interface (UI) of the app,

**3.** Connecting the UI components such as buttons, labels, textboxes, etc. to the Swift code,

**4.** Coding in Swift – the actual programming part

**5.** Building the project: this means creating the executable (file that actually runs on device or simulator). This is not difficult as it sounds; Xcode does the entire job with a single click,

**6.** Trying the app on a simulator,

**7.** Running the app on a real iOS device (optional),

**8.** Publishing the app on the iOS App Store (optional).

## 3.2. Creating a New Xcode Project

When you start Xcode, it gives you three choices as shown in Figure 3.1: i) Get started with a playground, ii) Create a new Xcode project and iii) Clone an existing project. Xcode offers a good method for learning Swift language using a concept called "playground" and we will go through this in detail in the next chapter. Now, we will develop our first project therefore let's choose to create a new project in Xcode (Second option in Figure 3.1 as shown by the arrow.). The last alternative is for opening an existing project from a repository but since this is your first project, this option does not apply.

Figure 3.1. Creating a new Xcode project for our first app

After you select "Create a new Xcode project", Xcode asks you what type of application you will create. Xcode is not only used for iOS development, it can also be used for developing Mac OS, watchOS and tvOS apps. For our iOS app, we need to select the iOS option from the top (shown inside the ellipse) and then a "Single View Application" (shown by the rectangle) as in Figure 3.2. "Single View Application" means that you will create an app which has only one screen (one page) and you won't use tabs to change screens, etc. Since our aim is to simply write "Hello, World!" in the middle of the screen, "Single View Application" does the job. After then please click "Next" (shown by the arrow).

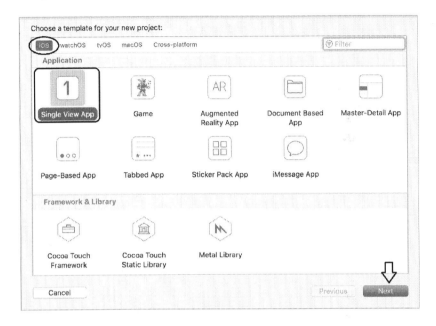

Figure 3.2. Creating a "Single View App"

## 3.3. Project Settings

Xcode now shows an options dialog box as in Figure 3.3. It asks for the "Product Name" (indicated by number 1). This will be the name of your app. We can fill in "Hello World" as shown in the figure. Of course you can give any name you like but it is a good practice to name your projects in such a way that you can guess what it does by just simply checking its name a few months later.

Next, the development team is selected by the drop down box (click the blue arrow at number 2). You'll see your name here since you set up signing before. It will automatically be available in the drop down box menu.

Then, you can enter an organization name (shown by number 3). This is optional; you may leave the organization name blank.

Next, the organization identifier is needed (shown by number 4). This is an essential information you should enter. It is generally in the form of com.yourname (like a reversed web address). Organization identifier is used to generate the "Bundle Identifier" shown beneath the organization identifier. This is used to distinguish among developers when you upload your app to the App Store. "Bundle Identifier" is automatically generated so you don't have to worry about it.

You can select between Objective-C (foregoing language) and Swift (new language) in the selection box shown in number 5. You are heading up for learning Swift so please select Swift there.

If you were patient enough to read until here, click next and then select the place where you want to save your Xcode project on your Mac as shown in Figure 3.4. I selected my Desktop but anywhere you like is OK. Then click "Create" as shown by the arrow in Figure 3.4.

Now you have created your project files and Xcode main screen appears as in Figure 3.5. In this window, you can view and change general properties of your project (section inside the ellipse). I'll not dive deep here and the defaults are OK for now. You don't need to change these settings for this project.

**Important note:** Xcode 9 may ask you to connect a real iOS device for setting up the signing identity for this project in the Signing section shown in Figure 3.5. In this case, please connect your iOS device to your Mac via the lightning cable and then try to select the signing identity while the real device is connected to your Mac.

## 3.4. Default Files of a New Project

At the left pane lies the list of the files and folders of your project (inside the rectangle in Figure 3.5). When you created your project, these files are automatically generated and saved at the location you indicated in Figure 3.4. File type is specified by the file extension as you probably know. I'd like to bring your attention towards the default files included in your project:

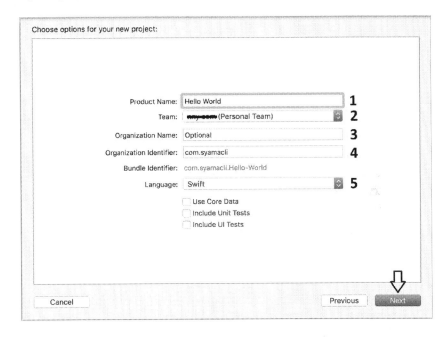

Figure 3.3. Setting options for your first project

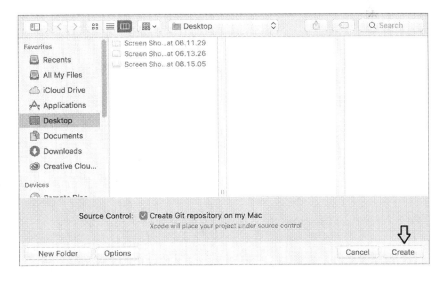

Figure 3.4. Selecting the place to save your Xcode project

**1.** Some files in your project have the extension of .swift and these files are Swift files. You write your Swift code in these files and make your app to do what it is supposed to do. AppDelegate.swift file determines how our app will talk to iOS while **ViewController.swift** is your main code file that will determine the behaviour of your controller (app) screen.

**2.** Some files have the extension of .storyboard. These files store the information regarding the user interface of your app such as where a button should be or what colour your screen background will be. Launchscreen.storyboard holds information that will be shown to the user while the app is being loaded (splash screen). **Main.storyboard** contains the layout of the main screen of your app.

**3.** There is a file called Assets.xcasseets. This file holds data, images, etc. that will be used by the app such as an app icon or a background image for your app.

**4.** There is another file called info.plist. This is a **property list** file and it contains the configuration data of the finalized executable such as copyright info, release date of the app or the device capabilities required to install the app.

You can view the contents of these files by single-clicking on them. When you click on files with the extension of .swift, Xcode shows an editor in the middle pane in which you can write Swift code inside. This editor has syntax highlighting and auto-completion properties that are really useful during coding. The ViewController.swift file is shown in Figure 3.6 as an example. Similarly when you click on the Main.storyboard as in Figure 3.7, Xcode shows an empty device screen in which you can place visual components like textboxes, buttons, etc.

**In short, you design the user interface of your app in .storyboard files while you write the required code in .swift files.**

## 3.5. Adding a Label Object

Let's see how you'll write "Hello, World" on the app screen. Firstly, single-click on the Main.storyboard file on the left pane of Xcode and the

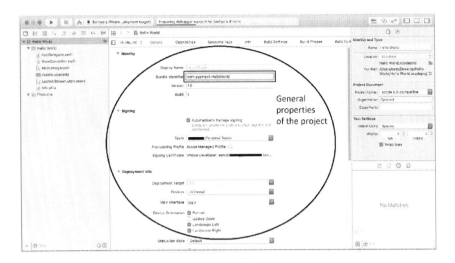

Figure 3.5 General properties of the project in Xcode

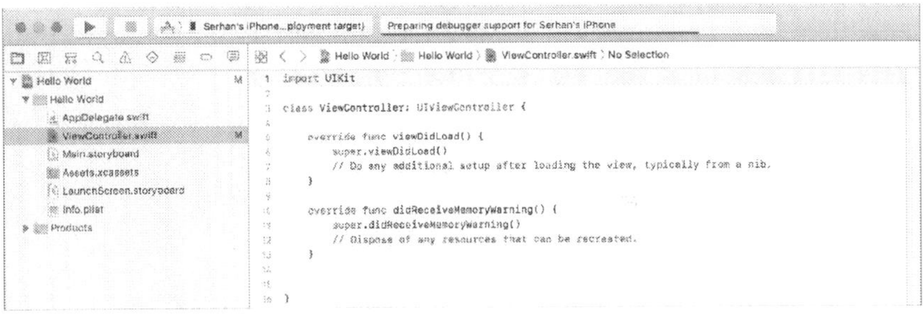

Figure 3.6. The "ViewController.swift" file of our app

main app layout will be displayed as in Figure 3.7. Here you can see that the selected device size is iPhone 8 as shown inside the small rectangle at the bottom. If you click on the "iPhone 8" text there, you can switch among all iOS device sizes such as iPhone 8 Plus, iPhone X, etc. In the bigger rectangle at the right bottom in this Figure, the so-called "object library" is shown. All available user interface objects that you can use in your app are shown in the object library. If you cannot see the object library, make sure that the "component menu selector" shown by the arrow (a circle with a small square inside) is selected.

"Label" objects are used to display text on the app screen. Xcode is very user-friendly, it shows small explanations of all components that you can use on the layout. You can find the component called "Label" manually from that menu or you can search for it by writing "Label" in the small search box just beneath that components menu. When you find the "Label" component, you can drag it and drop on the screen. I mean left-click on the label component, hold down the mouse button, drag it on the screen where you want to place it and then release the mouse button. If you try to place the "Label" in the middle of the screen, Xcode will help you by showing horizontal and vertical guiding lines as shown in Figure 3.8.

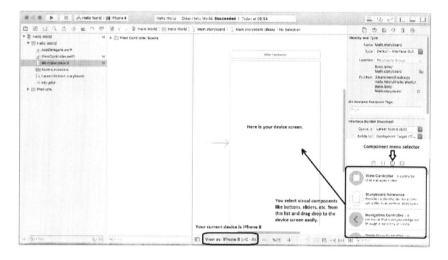

Figure 3.7. The "Main.storyboard" file of the project

After placing the "Label" component, it will be automatically selected. If not, single-click on it and it will be selected. Now, we can set the properties of this component. As you can see from Figure 3.9, the attributes of the selected "Label" component are shown in the right pane of Xcode. Please note that since a component has vast number of properties in Xcode, Xcode groups these properties for ease of view. In order to change the text properties of the "Label", select the "Attributes" group by clicking the fancy icon shown inside the small rectangle at top right in Figure 3.9. In this case, we are ready to change the text written inside the "Label" object. When you place a "Label" object on the screen, it automatically sets its text as "Label".

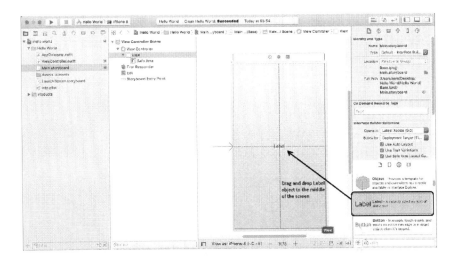

Figure 3.8. Placing a "Label" component on the screen

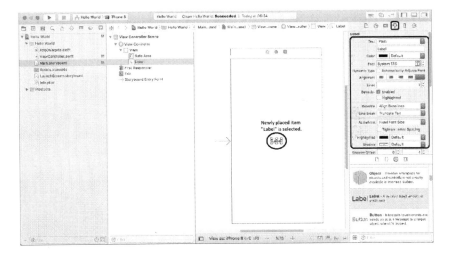

Figure 3.9. Changing the attributes of the "Label" object

We will now change its text to "Hello, World!". You can change the text from the second box in the right pane shown in Figure 3.9. It is "Label" by default; replace that text with "Hello, World!" (without quotation marks) or whatever you like to write on the app screen. After you change the text, hit Return on the keyboard. Now, the text should be changed as "Hello, World!" on the screen. If the text is too long compared to the Label's length, it may not be shown completely. In this case, you can

**drag one of the edges** of the Label component to fit the text inside it. In other words, stretch out the Label object so that you fit the text inside. Then, reposition the Label component in the middle of the screen with the help of guiding lines as before.

This process is summarized in Figure 3.10. The final screen layout of your app should be the one shown in the right image of Figure 3.10.

Since we don't want our first app to do something interactive, we don't need to write single line of code for now. Of course we'll do a lot of coding in the upcoming projects but for now, we don't need to do coding.

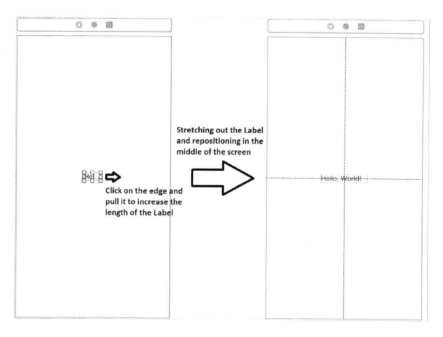

Figure 3.10. Final touches to our first app

## 3.6. Building the Project and Running on a Simulator

Your first app is now ready to be built in Xcode and run on a simulator or an actual device. This is easy in Xcode. Firstly, you have to select a simulator or device to run your app on. You can do this by clicking on the device or simulator name located at the left top of your Xcode window as shown in Figure 3.11. The iPhone 8 simulator is selected in this example but you can select any simulator you want or download more simulators which are also given as a choice in the selection menu (explained in detail in Chapter 2).

After selecting the simulator as shown inside the rectangle, the only thing you need to do is to press the "Run" button shown inside the circle in Figure 3.11. When you click the "Run" button, Xcode builds the project (makes the executable file), the device simulator starts running and boots like a real device. Note that this make take a while depending on your computer speed. After the simulator boots, it automatically installs the app you created and runs it as shown in Figure 3.12. **If you see the simulator screen shown in this figure, congratulations. You've successfully created your first iOS 11 app.**

Figure 3.11. Selecting a simulator or device to run your first app

In order to change anything in your app, you can press the "Stop" button which is next to the "Play" button in Xcode. After stopping the app, the simulator won't shut down completely but it will stop running your app. Then you can make any modification you want in your app such as changing the position of the Label component or the text you've written inside it. After changes, restart the simulator again by the "Run" button. As you can see from your very first project, Xcode provides a user-friendly interface and vast number of possibilities for transforming your ideas into real iOS apps.

Figure 3.12. Simulator screen showing our "Hello, World!" app

## 3.7. Running on a Real Device

It is also easy to try your app on a real iOS device. In order to do that, you just need to connect your device to your Mac using the lightning cable. Xcode will automatically detect and show it in the available devices as shown in Figure 3.13. I connected my iPhone but you can run the app on any compatible iOS device. Note that, you can run your apps on a device connected to your Mac but you cannot distribute it for installing on other devices, you need to join Apple Developer Program for that.

Figure 3.13. Selecting a real device in Xcode

After selecting the device, hit the "Run" button to install the app on the device. Xcode will give an error as shown in Figure 3.14. It says that you should allow running apps from this developer on your device. As the error box says, navigate to General → Device Management and click "trust the developer profile" on the device. After that, you can run your apps on your device.

Figure 3.14. Error dialog in Xcode about running the app on a real device

After allowing on your device, hit the "Run" button in Xcode again to run it. If you see the "Hello, World!" text on the real device, excellent. You now know how to install apps on real iOS devices. Running an app on an actual device is sometimes essential since some operations like SMS sending can only be done on real devices.

**Final note:** If the iOS version on your device is lower than iOS 11, then Xcode will issue an error and won't run the app on the device. In order to solve this, you should either update the device OS to iOS 11 or change the iOS version of your app to match the iOS version of your device. For example, if you're using a device with iOS 10, you can make your app compatible with iOS 10 from the main project menu as shown in Figure 3.15.

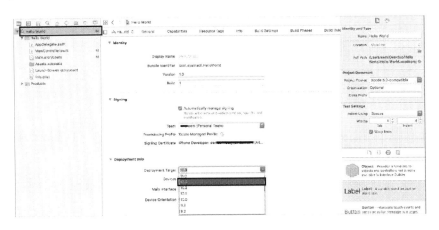

Figure 3.15. Changing the iOS compatibility of the app in Xcode

# Chapter 4

## SWIFT BASICS

### 4.1. Introduction to Playgrounds

We have created our first app. Great. But as you may have noticed, we didn't have any interaction with it. It just writes a text on the screen and that's it. In order to make an app to do something, we need to tell it what to do. And we need to tell it exactly.

As an old saying states: "Computers are actually rather stupid". This is because: **if you're telling a computer to do a task, then you need to tell it in exact terms. The operation principles of computers are different than those of humans.** Let's try to explain this by an example: imagine that you're going home after a tiring workday and your wife is already at home. You want to have a pizza for the dinner and ring her for baking a frozen pizza. A usual form of conversation would be like the following:

You – Hi darling, hope you're OK.

Your wife – Thanks, a bit tired. You?

You – Me too. And also hungry as a wolf. Didn't have a bit since lunch. Could you bake a pizza for me? There should be some frozen pizzas in the fridge.

Your wife – Of course, I'll. See you in a while, bye.

You – Thanks, bye.

Then, she'll find the pizza wherever it is in the fridge, unpack it, set the timer, power on the microwave and bake it. That's it. However, if you had a robot wife with a computer brain, the dialog would be more like this:

You – Hi darling, hope you're OK.

Robot wife – I'm OK, just charged. You OK? (not in a romantic tone!)

You – Thanks. I'm tired and hungry. Could you bake a pizza for me please, I guess there are some in the fridge.

Robot wife – Where are the pizzas in fridge, what type of pizza do you want: margherita, pizza with egg, etc., do you want it crispy? When do you want it to be ready?....

You – Stop, stop please. I'll drive to a restaurant.

Robot wife – I don't understand, you are nonsense....

Well, any programmable digital device is more or less the same. **You have to tell exact things to them.** You do this by using programming languages. There are a lot of different programming languages used to develop software for different platforms. You can check the widely used programming languages and their rankings at the TIOBE index website: http://www.tiobe.com/tiobe-index/. It is sometimes difficult to choose which programming language to use. There is not a universally excellent/complete programming language; they have strong and weak sides. On the other hand, another good thing about Apple is that they design both software and hardware in such a way that you don't get confused. The same is valid for their programming languages.

The main programming language for Mac OS and iOS devices had been Objective-C before Swift came into play. Objective-C can still be used to create apps. However, Swift is the newer technology and its popularity is constantly rising. Moreover, Swift took over Objective-C in the TIOBE index in September 2016.

Apple developed Swift and introduced it in 2014 WWDC (World Wide Developers Conference). Swift was a proprietary language then, but in 2015 Apple made it open-source software. You can view the evolution of Swift on its official website: https://swift.org.

Important changes were made in Swift since its introduction. Swift 2 and Swift 3 came in 2015 and 2016; and in September 2017, the fourth version of Swift: Swift 4 is released. Please note that these major versions are not fully compatible with each other.

In this chapter, you will learn the basics of Swift 4. It is worth noting that learning everything of a programming language is almost impossible nowadays but learning its logic and the syntax is the first step. You can improve your knowledge easily once you grasp the basics.

In the previous chapter, you learned that it is possible to write Swift code inside the files with the extension ".swift" in an Xcode project. You can then build the project to try on a simulator or a device. In this case, you will need to do the modify-build-run cycle each time you change something in the Swift code. Since this is a time consuming process for learning a new programming language, Xcode offers something better to replace this cycle: Swift Playgrounds. In Swift Playgrounds, you can see the output of your code in real time as you type without the need of the modify-build-run cycle.

We will use playgrounds in this chapter since our aim is not creating an app now, we'll focus on the syntax and the logic of Swift 4. In order to do this, we need to create a new playground file. We can do this by selecting the "Get started with a playground" button that appears when you run Xcode first time as pointed out by the arrow in Figure 4.1 or you can select File → New → Playground from the top toolbar of Xcode. It will ask you to choose a template which will be **iOS** and **Blank** and then enter the filename and the location to save the file on your Mac. You can give any name to your file. When created, the default Xcode playground looks like in Figure 4.2.

Figure 4.1. Creating a new playground file to try Swift code

Figure 4.2. The default playground just after we create it

As you can see from Figure 4.2, Xcode places three default lines of code when you create a new playground. The first line is:

```
//: Playground - noun: a place where people can play
```
Code 4.1

This is a comment line. It defines what a playground is. In fact, this is not an actual code. It is a comment for you to read and get an idea about what's going on in these code lines. Xcode ignores comment lines when it builds an app from your code. Comments exist in almost all programming languages and their aim is to make people understand the code easier. In Swift, a comment can be a single line as above or several lines if you need. For a single line comment, // is used. Xcode will consider that all the text written after **//** is a part of the comment and will ignore whatever you write after **//** in that line.

The next line is:

```
import UIKit
```
Code 4.2

This line is used to import a library called UIKit. There are loads of libraries in iOS software development kit (SDK) and they provide ready to use functions that help us to develop apps. Libraries should be imported in our Swift code before we can use the functions or classes belonging to those libraries. The keyword **import** enables us to include libraries in our code.

In the above line, a framework called **UIKit** is imported. Xcode automatically places this line of code on top of playground files because UIKit contains the main framework for the user interface.

The last line is

```
var str = "Hello, playground"
```
Code 4.3

In this line, a variable named "str" is defined. Variables are entities that hold information. You can think them as boxes that you put and get data into and from them. There are several types of boxes sorry; types of variables exist in Swift.

One of the widely used variable types is the **string. A string holds a group of characters.** For example, the word "example" is a string since it is composed of characters "e", "x", "a", "m", "p", "l", "e". Similarly, the following is also a string: "Swift 4" since it is composed of the following characters: "S", "w", "i", "f", "t", " ", "4". Note that the space between "t" and "4" is also counted as a character. In our playground, a variable called "str" is created and it holds the string of "Hello, playground". This is a simple line but also an important line. It shows the basic structure of variable declaration in Swift. You'll see various variable types in the next subsection.

It is important to note that Swift keywords such as **var** and **import** are automatically coloured in Xcode to increase the readability of the code.

The unique property of a playground is that it shows the contents of variables immediately in the right pane. For example, consider the output of the playground file as shown inside the rectangle in Figure 4.2. In that output, Xcode says that: "The variable you created has this value: "Hello, playground" ". In other words, Xcode shows the content of the newly created variable. This makes it easy for us to follow the variable across our code. If you change the value of the variable "str" to something else later, Xcode will also show that next to the related code line.

We'll learn more on variables in the following subsection.

## 4.2. Variables in Swift

As just stated, variables can be thought as boxes that hold data. Firstly, you create these boxes: this is called "declaration of variables". You can insert the data which will be held by the variable during the declaration or later, it is up to you.

Just as real world boxes that can be used to hold different things like a sugar box, a match box or a component box, **variables in Swift also have different types**. For example, if you want to store a numeric data (a number) in a variable, the type of the variable should be Integer. If you don't specify the variable type, Xcode will automatically guess its type. Let's explain this on a simple example. Please consider the following code line:

```
var myNumber = 3
```
Code 4.4

In this line, we declare a variable called "myNumber" using the keyword **var** and assign the number 3 to this variable using the assignment operator: **=** (the equal sign). Xcode automatically colours the value that will be assigned to the variable. In this code, we made both **a declaration and an assignment**. We declared the variable name and assigned 3. Since this is an integer value (a whole number that doesn't have fractional part), Xcode will automatically set the type of this variable as Integer (shortly: Int). If you want to be in full control of the type of your variable (which is a good practice in programming), then you can explicitly specify its type during declaration as follows:

```
var myNumber: Int = 3
```
Code 4.5

In this code, you tell Xcode that your variable will have the type **Int** (Integer) and you want to assign the value 3 to this variable during declaration as sketched in Figure 4.3.

Another way of declaring the variable "myNumber" and **then** assigning its value is as follows:

```
var myNumber: Int
//Some other code here...
myNumber = 3
```
Code 4.6

In the first line, we declared the variable myNumber first but didn't assign a value. Because of this, Xcode cannot guess the type of the variable therefore we are required to define the type of the variable. Otherwise, Xcode will issue an error. After the declaration of the variable, we may have some other code. And then we assigned the value 3 to your variable in the third line. Declaring a variable and assigning its value later may be useful when its value will be calculated in the code.

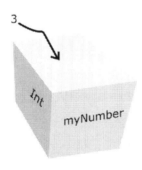

Figure 4.3. Assigning 3 to the variable "myNumber"

When we create the variable "myNumber" and assign its value, the playground shows the value in the right pane as in Figure 4.4.

Figure 4.4. Declaration and assignment of a variable

It is worth repeating that the equal sign, **=**, is called as the "assignment operator" in Swift. It assigns the value at its right to the variable placed at its left. In the above example, the value 3 is assigned to the variable named "myNumber".

Another widely used variable type in Swift is the **string** as stated before. Strings are anything composed of characters. Assigning the word "Hello" to a string variable is shown below:

```
var myString: String = "Hello"
```
Code 4.7

Note that the value we want to assign is written inside quotation marks. This is a rule for assigning a string.

The code shown below may confuse you a bit:

```
var myNewString: String = "3"
```
Code 4.8

In this code, we assigned "3" to "myNewString". The "3" here is not a number. It is a string because it is written in quotation marks. Anything inside quotation marks will be treated as a string by Swift. Let's have a look at the output of our playground file in Figure 4.5.

Note that, playground output shows "3" inside quotation marks. This means that it uses this variable as a string.

Figure 4.5. Declaration of a string

If you define an integer and try to assign a string value to it as in Code 4.9, you get an error:

```
var myWrongNumber: Int = "3"
```
Code 4.9

Xcode shows the erroneous code line as in Figure 4.6. It places an exclamation mark at the left of the wrong code (indicated by the arrow in the figure). If you single-click on the exclamation mark, Xcode shows further explanation about what's wrong with your code as shown inside the rectangle in Figure 4.6.

Figure 4.6. Wrong assignment to an integer variable

Other frequently used variable types are the **double** and **float**. They hold decimal numbers and very useful if you need to store any sort of number having decimal point such as 3,14 or 27,6935.

The difference between **double** and **float** types is the number of decimal digits they can hold. You can see their difference by trying Code 4.10 in the playground.

```
var myDouble: Double = 3.12345678901234567890
var myFloat: Float = 3.12345678901234567890
```
Code 4.10

In the above code, we are trying to assign a decimal number with 20 decimal digits to a double and float variable. Let's check what Xcode gets from these assignments:

41

Figure 4.7. Double and float assignments in Xcode

It can easily be seen that Xcode takes 15 decimal digits for the **double** type and 6 digits for the **float** type (see the output of the playground file above). Considering that iOS devices have big amount of RAMs, it is better to define decimal numbers in **double** type. If you don't specify the type of a decimal assignment, Xcode automatically treats it as a **double** type variable anyway.

Another useful and widely used variable type is the **boolean**. This variable type takes two values only: **true** or **false**. You can think it as a yes-no question like "Is the screen background red?". The answer can only be "yes" or "no". Instead of the words "yes" and "no", Swift uses **true** and **false**.

Assignment of a boolean variable is also simple as shown below:

```
var myBoolean: Bool = true
```
Code 4.11

You'll see the importance of Boolean variables when you start to code apps that have complex logic inside.

We have studied simple variable types so far. These types are called as "primitive" types since they are used for storing single data at a time whether it is an integer, string, etc. In Swift, as in other programming languages, there are also complex variable types that hold groups of data. Arrays, dictionaries and sets are the widely used ones among complex types and these will be covered here.

Arrays store multiple values of the same type in an ordered fashion. A typical array can be illustrated as in Figure 4.8.

| Index | Value |
|-------|-------------|
| 0 | "Tea" |
| 1 | "Coffee" |
| 2 | "Sandwich" |
| 3 | "Chocolate" |
| 4 | "Pizza" |

Figure 4.8. Contents of a typical array

Array elements have indices so that you can access them, delete them or replace them. Indices of arrays always start with 0 and increase one by one. In order to declare the array shown above, we use the following code:

```
var myArray: [String] = ["Tea", "Coffee", "Sandwich",
"Chocolate", "Pizza"]
```
Code 4.12

We can access each element in our array using the following template: myArray[index]. The following code accesses first and fourth elements of the array we just formed:

```
myArray[0]     //First element
myArray[3]     //Fourth element
```
Code 4.13

We can change any element of our array using a simple assignment as follows:

```
myArray[3]   = "Cola"
```
Code 4.14

The 4th element of our array is changed from "Chocolate" to "Cola" by this code. After this line, if we just write the name of your array in the playground, it will show our array as **["Tea", "Coffee", "Sandwich", "Cola", "Pizza"]**.

We can remove any element using the following pattern:

```
myArray.remove( at: 3)
```
Code 4.15

This line removes the element at the 4$^{th}$ position. After this modification, our array has the following structure: **["Tea", "Coffee", "Sandwich", "Pizza"]**.

We can append a new element to our array as follows:

```
myArray.append("IceTea")
```
Code 4.16

After this line, our array owns **"IceTea"** as its last element: **["Tea", "Coffee", "Sandwich", "Pizza", "IceTea"]**. All of these operations and their results are shown below:

Figure 4.9. Basic array operations in Swift

Finally, let's see how we can define an empty array:

```
var myIntArray = [Int] ()
```
Code 4.17

Arrays are really useful while dealing with chunks of data of the same type. For example if we want to log (save) our geolocation data read from GPS by regular time intervals, we can use an array consisting of **double** type elements.

Another useful complex variable type is the "dictionary". Dictionaries hold elements as a **key-value pair**. Let's form a dictionary of the exam results of a student. His points were as follows: Maths: 8, Physics: 9, Chemistry: 7, Programming: 10. We can illustrate these results as in Figure 4.10 which shows a dictionary structure. The **keys** are the strings that are names of the lectures and the **values** are the exam points the student got.

| Key | Value |
|---|---|
| Maths | 8 |
| Physics | 9 |
| Chemistry | 7 |
| Programming | 10 |

Figure 4.10. Exam results of a student

We can define a dictionary from this table as follows:

```
var examResults = ["Maths" : 8 , "Physics" : 9,
"Chemistry" : 7, "Programming" : 10]
```
Code 4.18

After defining the dictionary, we can query (ask) the value corresponding to a key. If we write "examResults["Physics"]" in the playground, Xcode will output the value for the "Physics" key as shown below:

Figure 4.11. Declaring and querying a dictionary in Swift

Replacing the value in a dictionary is very similar to changing the elements of an array. The following code changes the value of "Physics" to 10.

```
examResults["Physics"] = 10
```
Code 4.19

We can also remove a key-value pair as shown in Code 4.19. Please note the form of the method we need to apply is: **removeValue(forKey : (the key of the entry to be removed))**.

```
examResults.removeValue(forKey : "Chemistry")
```
Code 4.20

After all these changes, if we just write the name of the dictionary (examResults) in our playground, Xcode will show the contents of our dictionary as shown below:

Figure 4.12. Basic dictionary operations

The third important complex variable type is the "set". Sets have two unique properties: i) they hold data of the same type without an order; ii) an element can only be added to a set only once. In other words, the same value can only appear once in a set. Let's create a set of strings as an example. We can create a set of fruits and then insert a new element as shown below:

```
var fruits: Set<String> = ["Strawberry", "Banana",
"Peach", "Apricot"]
fruits.insert("Mango")
```
Code 4.21

If we just write "fruits" (name of the set) in the playground, Xcode will show the contents of the set in the right pane as: {"Mango", "Banana", "Apricot", "Strawberry", "Peach"}.

We can think sets as a magic bag. When we throw in an element that already exists, one of them vanishes. Let's try to insert the element "Banana" again to the set as below:

```
fruits.insert("Banana")
```
Code 4.22

Xcode will not issue a warning or an error but if we again check the contents of "fruits" set, Xcode will show {"Mango", "Banana", "Apricot", "Strawberry", "Peach"}, which is the same as before adding "Banana" the second time. Hence, only one instance of an element can exist inside a set. Sets are useful for checking if one of several conditions is met in a complex app. The playground page of basic set operations is given in Figure 4.13.

Figure 4.13. Creating and manipulating a set in Swift

In summary, we have learned following variable types that are widely used in Swift:

**1. Primitive types:** integer, string, double, float, boolean.

**2. Complex types:** array, dictionary, set.

**Warning:** Swift is case-sensitive, "myNumber" is not the same as "mynumber", so be careful about naming and calling your variables.

Apart from regular variables, there are two related concepts: "optionals" and "constants".

"Optionals" are the variables that may not contain data. It may seem awkward at first glance but it is true and sometimes very useful. We define an optional but we may or may not place a value in it. We can think of optionals as an empty box. If we ask its value before assigning a value, Swift will show its value as "nil" meaning nothing or empty. If we place a value inside an optional and then ask its content, Swift will return whatever it contains as a regular variable.

A real-world example is the middle name. Not everybody should have a middle name. Some people have and some not. If we need variables to hold initial name, middle name and surname as strings in Swift, **we could try** to do this by the following code:

```
var initialName: String = "John"
var middleName: String
var surname: String = "Smith"
print(initialName)
print(middleName)
print(surname)
```
Code 4.23

Xcode will give an error in this code because the variable "middleName" is declared but not assigned a value before trying to print it on the 5th line.

If we define the "middleName" variable as an optional, Xcode will not issue an error. Optionals are declared with a question mark (?) at the end of the declaration as shown in Code 4.24. The optional "middleName" is defined but not assigned a value. In this case, Swift automatically sets its value to "nil". Xcode shows "nil" when we try to print the value of "middleName" as shown in Figure 4.14.

```
var initialName: String = "John"
var middleName: String?
var surname: String = "Smith"
print(initialName)
print(middleName)
print(surname)
```
Code 4.24

After we assign a value to an optional (also called as wrapping the optional) as in Code 4.25, we can then print its value by unwrapping it (reading its value). **An exclamation mark (!) is used for reading the value of an optional as given in Code 4.25.** The Xcode output for this code is also shown in Figure 4.15.

Figure 4.14. Printing the value of an empty optional

```
var initialName: String = "John"
var middleName: String?
var surname: String = "Smith"
print(initialName)
middleName = "Doe"      //optional wrapped
print(middleName!)      //optional unwrapped
print(surname)
```
Code 4.25

Figure 4.15. Wrapping and unwrapping an optional

Another important keyword in Swift is the **let** keyword. We can define **constants** (data that will be assigned once and will not change ever in your code) using **let**. We just use **let** instead of **var** keyword for defining a constant; type definition and assignment process are the same as regular variables as shown the following code:

```
let SPEED_LIMIT_MWAY = 70    // speed limit = 70 mph for
                             // all motorways
let SPEED_LIMIT_RA = 30      // speed limit = 30 mph for
                             //restricted areas
print("Speed limit in motorways
is: \(SPEED_LIMIT_MWAY), speed limit in roads with
traffic lights is \(SPEED_LIMIT_RA)")
```
Code 4.26

In this code, **print()** function prints the string inside the parentheses in the right pane of the playground. It is a very handy function to track your code. Please note that numeric values are printed using the **\()** operator inside the **print()** function. Constant declaration in the playground is also shown in Figure 4.16.

Some programmers use all capital letters to define constants so that they will remember these are constants in their code as we did for our example here.

If we try to re-assign a value to a constant, Swift will throw an error which is shown in Figure 4.17. Hence, we have to be extra careful when using constants. **Assign once and never assign again, don't ever try** ☺.

Figure 4.16. Defining constants in Swift

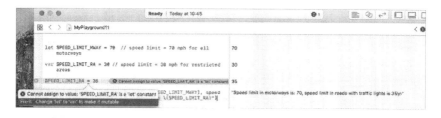

Figure 4.17. Trying to change the value of a constant

The next subject is the logical decision making structures in Swift, let's have a coffee break and then continue with if-else statements.

## 4.3. Logical Decision Making Statements in Swift

Logical decision making is one of the main concepts in programming languages, like in real-world problems. In daily life, we make a lot of logical decisions such as:

- "**If** their pizza is tasty, I'll order again next week, **else** I'll not order from them again".

- "**If** it's sunny I'll go for a walk, **else** I'll stay home".

Just like in daily life, an if-else statements basically checks if a condition is met or not in a programming language. If the condition is met, the code inside the **if block** is executed. If the condition isn't met, then the code in the **else block** is executed. Hence, if we wanted to tell the above sunny – not sunny example to the computer, we would do it like this:

if it's sunny {

      I'll go for a walk

}

else {

    I'll stay home

}

Let's see how we can check if two numbers are equal in Swift using an if-else statement:

```
var myNumber1 = 3
var myNumber2 = 3
if (myNumber1 == myNumber2) {
    print("These numbers are equal.")
}
else {
    print("These numbers aren't equal.")
}
```
Code 4.27

In this code, two variables, **myNumber1** and **myNumber2**, are defined. Both variables are assigned the value of 3 during declaration. Then, an **if** statement checks if **myNumber1** is equal to **myNumber2**. The operator **==** checks if these contents of these variables are equal. If they are equal, the condition of the **if** statement is met therefore the code inside the **if block** is executed. If they are not equal, then the code inside the **else block** is executed. Note that these blocks are specified by curly braces. Since the two numbers are equal, the code inside the **if block** will be executed as you shown below:

Figure 4.18. If-else statement example in Swift

If we change one of the numbers to something different than 3, then the code inside the **else block** will be executed. This is also shown below:

Figure 4.19. If-else statement in Swift when the condition isn't met

We can also use several if-else statements in a nested form as in Code 4.28. In this code, the conditions are checked from top to down. If a condition is met, then the code inside its block is executed and the program ends. If none of the conditions are true, then it means that **myNumber1** is lower than **myNumber2** and the statement in the final **else** block is executed. **In other words, the statements in the last else block is executed if none of the conditions above it are met.** The screenshot of this nested code in the playground is given in Figure 4.20.

```swift
var myNumber1 = 1
var myNumber2 = 3
if (myNumber1 == myNumber2) {
    print("These numbers are equal.")
}
else if (myNumber1 > myNumber2){
    print("myNumber1 is greater than myNumber2.")
}
else {
    print("myNumber1 is lower than myNumber2.")
}
```
Code 4.28

Figure 4.20. Nested if-else statements in Swift

Nested if-else statements may become confusing as more and more conditions are added. In order to check several conditions easier, **switch-case** statements are used. Switch-case statements function similar to nested if-else blocks but they are less error-prone for coding multiple numbers of conditions. A switch-case example is given in Code 4.29. The variable to be checked is written next to the `switch` keyword. In this example, the content of the variable "temperature" is checked. In each `case` statement, the "temperature" variable is checked against their condition. For example, in the first `case` statement, temperature is checked if it meets the condition of "-40..<0". In Swift 4, the statement `a..<b` means: "between a and b (a is included, b is not included in the comparison)". Hence, if temperature is between -40 and 0, then the statement inside the "case -40..<0:" condition is executed which is `print("It's very cold.")`. Each `case` statement is checked one by one from top to down. If none of the conditions inside the given case statements are met, then the code inside the `default` block is executed.

```
var temperature = 22
switch temperature {
case -40..<0:
    print("It's very cold.")
case 0..<15:
    print("It's cold.")
case 15..<30:
    print("It's nice")
case 30..<40:
    print("It's hot")
default:
    print("It's either too cold or too hot.")
}
```
Code 4.29

In Swift, switch cases must be "exhaustive" meaning that you have to cover all possibilities regarding the switched variable. Since it is usually difficult to cover all values for data types except the Boolean, the inclusion of a default case is almost mandatory. In the code above, the temperature variable is assigned 22. This value is between 15 and 30 therefore the condition of the third `case` statement is satisfied. In this case, the program outputs the text "It's nice." as shown below:

Figure 4.21. Switch-case statement in Swift

If we change the temperature, then the program will check it again and output a different text accordingly as in Figure 4.22.

Figure 4.22. Switch-case: another condition is met

We'll use decision making statements extensively. Let's now move on to another important subject: loops.

## 4.4. Loops in Swift

Performing the same operation in a repeated manner is a frequently needed concept in programming. We do these repetitions using loops. Without loops, programming would be almost impossible. For example, let's try to find the sum of numbers from 1 to 20. Without loops, we would do this as follows:

```
var sum = 0
sum = sum + 1
sum = sum + 2
sum = sum + 3
.... (16 more lines of code here)
sum = sum + 19
sum = sum + 20
```

Code 4.30

Please note that there are 16 more lines of code in the place shown by dots (shortened above). Therefore, this simple task takes 21 lines of code. And it's error prone. Remember that we want to do things with shortest code possible to prevent errors. Below, we'll see how we can obtain the sum of these numbers with loops in a shorter and more elegant way.

There are two main looping methods in Swift. First of them is the loop structure using the **for** keyword. The basic structure of the **for** loop is given below:

```
for (sweep elements) {
    (code to be repeated)
}
```
Code 4.31

In this snippet, the **(code to be repeated)** is repeated again and again as long as the there's a remaining element in the **(sweep elements)**. In order to explain this in a better way, let's calculate the sum of the numbers from 1 to 20 using the **for** loop as in Code 4.32. In this code, the expression **1...20** is a range structure. In each iteration of the **for loop**, the loop variable called **counter** takes one value from the range **1...20**. In this way, the counter takes the values of **1, 2, 3, 4, ..., 18, 19, 20** one by one. In each iteration (i.e. for each value of the **counter** variable), the expression inside the loop: **sum = sum + counter** is executed. Since the declared variable **sum** is initialized to zero before the loop, the expression inside the loop adds the numbers from 1 to 20 and stores the sum in the variable **sum**. In the end, the expression **print(sum)** just outputs the sum variable in the playground as in Figure 4.23.

```
var sum = 0
for counter in 1...20 {
    sum = sum + counter
}
print(sum)
```
Code 4.32

As it is seen from Figure 4.23, the sum of the numbers from 1 to 20 is calculated as 210.

Figure 4.23. **for** loop in Swift

**Note:** As it is stated above, the expression **start_num...end_num** means that all the numbers from **start_num** to **end_num** will be included in the loop. If it is **1...5**, the for loop will be repeated for **1, 2, 3, 4, 5**. It is also possible to not to include the **end_num**. If we write the loop sweep as **1..<5**, it means that 5 is not included and the loop variable will take the values of **1, 2, 3 and 4**.

We can use other variable types as the loop variable, not just numbers. For example, let's to access the elements of an array using a **for** loop as shown in the following code:

```swift
var myArray: [Character] = ["S", "w", "i", "f", "t"]
for myChar in myArray {
    print(myChar)
}
```
Code 4.33

In this code, we have defined an array of characters composed of the letters of the word "Swift". Then we access the elements of this array with a **for** loop. We print its characters one by one as we sweep them. We can see the output of the print statement at the bottom of the playground as below:

Figure 4.24. Accessing array elements using a **for** loop

The other looping structure in Swift is the **while** loop. It is very similar to the **for** loop. The main difference of the **while** loop is as that the incrementing method of the loop variable is specified inside the loop therefore it provides a bit more flexibility. The calculation of the sum of numbers from 1 to 20 using a **while** loop is shown in Code 4.34. In this code, the loop variable is also defined as a separate variable: **counter** before the loop begins. The **while** loop will be executed as long as **counter < 21** condition is satisfied. When **counter** becomes equal or greater than 21, the loop will quit. In order to increment the loop variable, the expression **counter = counter+1** is added inside the loop.

```
var counter = 0
var sum = 0
while counter < 21 {
    counter = counter + 1
    sum = sum + counter
}
print(sum)
```
Code 4.34

If we don't change the loop variable inside the loop, the loop continues forever making it an **infinite loop** which is a big trouble in programming. When a program goes into an infinite loop, it probably won't respond to user intervention and will crash a while later. Hence, always remember to change the loop variable in a **while** loop in such a way that your loop will quit after a finite number of executions.

The result of the **while** loop of is shown in the following figure:

Figure 4.25. **while** loop in Swift

The advantage of a **while** loop is that the increment of the loop variable can easily be controlled by the programmer. For example, if we wanted to increment the loop variable by 2 (which means calculating the sum of the odd numbers in the range of 1...20), we could just change the loop variable as **counter=counter+2**. In this case, the loop will add odd numbers in the range of 1-20 (1, 3, 5, ..., 17, 19) as in Figure 4.26.

Figure 4.26. Adding odd numbers with a **while** loop

In addition to the regular usage of the **for** and **while** loops as shown above, there are two Swift commands that provide further control of loops. These are **break** and **continue** keywords.

These commands are generally used together with an **if** statement. The **break** command breaks the loop, in other words the program quits the current loop before the loop condition expires. On the other hand the **continue** keyword makes the loop continue, i.e., the loop doesn't execute statements inside the loop block for the current value of the loop variable but continues with the next iteration.

## 4.5. Functions in Swift

Functions enable us to write programs with reduced number of repetitions. In other words, we can put the repeating code in function blocks. Let's clarify this by an example. Consider the code shown below that prints the elements of a character string using a **for** loop:

```
var myCharArray: [Character] = ["F", "u", "n", "c"]
for myChar in myCharArray {
    print(myChar)
}
```
Code 4.35

If we wanted to print the contents of the array ["F", "u", "n", "c"] 3 times, we would use Code 4.36. As the number of times we want to print increases, the code length increases proportionally. The number of total code lines would reach hundreds easily for a middle sized program with a lot of repetitions.

```
var myCharArray: [Character] = ["F", "u", "n", "c"]
for myChar in myCharArray {
    print(myChar)
}
for myChar in myCharArray {
    print(myChar)
}
for myChar in myCharArray {
    print(myChar)
}
```
Code 4.36

We can shorten this process by placing the repeating code inside a function. A function is defined with the **func** keyword in Swift as shown in Code 4.37. In this code, we defined a function called **repeatMyLoop**: this is the name of our function. The contents of a function are written inside curly braces. The array definition and the **for** loop for printing the elements of the array are placed inside this function.

```
func repeatMyLoop () {
var myCharArray: [Character] = ["F", "u", "n", "c"]
    for myChar in myCharArray {
        print(myChar)
                              }
                  }
```
Code 4.37

When we write this function in the playground, nothing shows at the output as seen in Figure 4.27 because **we defined the function but didn't call it**. Our function just stays there ready to be called. A function executes when it is called.

We call the function by shouting his name, sorry writing its name as shown in Figure 4.28. In this example, we have called the function **repeatMyLoop()** 3 times and it did its duty: created the array and printed its elements. Once we define a function, we can call it as many times as we want.

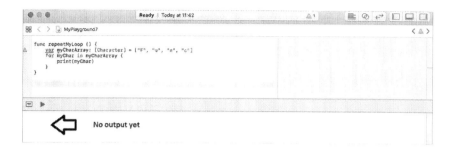

Figure 4.27. Function definition in Swift

As you may have noticed, the function is defined and called with regular parentheses. In the above example, inside of these parentheses is empty. We can define **parameters (inputs, arguments)** in these parentheses and use these parameters inside the function. In other words, we can pass any variable to a function as an input.

Figure 4.28. Calling our function 3 times

As an example, let's define a function that takes the raw price (price before tax) of a product and prints the selling price (price after tax). We can take the tax fixed at 8% for now. The function definition is as follows:

```
func printTaxed (priceBeforeTax: Double) {
    var priceAfterTax: Double = priceBeforeTax * 1.08
    print(priceAfterTax)
}
```
Code 4.38

In this definition, the function takes the variable **priceBeforeTax** as the input and this input is expected in Double type. Then, it calculates the taxed price inside by multiplying the **priceBeforeTax** by 1.08 (since the tax is 8%, price after tax = price before tax + 0.08*price before tax = 1.08*price before tax). The taxed price is stored in the variable called **priceAfterTax**. Finally, this variable is printed. We can calculate the taxed price of three different products easily by calling this function and giving the prices of items as inputs to the function as follows:

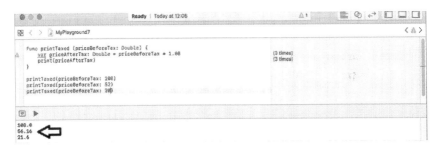

Figure 4.29. Passing inputs to a function

A function can take any number of parameters, not just one. In our example, we can also specify the tax rate since tax rate may be different for different products. In this case, we simply specify two inputs separated by a comma as shown below:

```
func printTaxed (priceBeforeTax: Double, taxRate: Double)
{
    var priceAfterTax: Double = priceBeforeTax *
(1+taxRate/100)
    print(priceAfterTax)
}
printTaxed(priceBeforeTax: 100, taxRate: 8)
printTaxed(priceBeforeTax: 52, taxRate: 8)
printTaxed(priceBeforeTax: 20, taxRate: 10)
```
Code 4.39

In this code, the formula priceAfterTax = priceBeforeTax * (1+taxRate/100) is used since the **taxRate** is considered as a percentage. In function calls, both the prices before taxes and tax rates should be provided as inputs.

Assume that we want to calculate the selling prices for three products. Two of these products have the prices of 100 and 52 with the tax rate of 8% while one product has the price of 20 and the tax rate of 10%. We can do these calculations using our function as follows:

Figure 4.30. Functions with multiple parameters (inputs)

Functions in Swift do not only accept inputs (function parameters, arguments) but they can also have outputs that can be assigned to other variables in the main code. Let's get the selling price as an output from our new function **getTaxed** as shown below:

```
func getTaxed (priceBeforeTax: Double, taxRate: Double)
-> Double {
    var priceAfterTax: Double = priceBeforeTax *
(1+taxRate/100)
    return priceAfterTax
}
print(getTaxed(priceBeforeTax: 100, taxRate: 8))
```
Code 4.40

In this function, the output of the function is a Double type therefore the function definition is closed with **a -> Double** expression. The function outputs the **priceAfterTax** variable with the **return** keyword. Therefore, this function accepts 2 Double type variables as inputs and it outputs a new Double type variable. This is shown in Figure 4.31.

We can use the output of our function in any way Swift allows. For example, we can print it as shown in Code 4.40 and Figure 4.32 or assign the output to another variable.

Figure 4.31. Our function's input and output structure

Figure 4.32. Printing the output of our new function "getTaxed"

As you have learned in this subsection, functions provide us a good way of shortening our code and making it compact. They are also important to share code among developers. If you can find a ready-coded function on the Internet, you can easily use it in your app. Hence, functions provide a good way of sharing code among developers. As stated before, iOS SDK has a lot of ready functions. You'll see how convenient it is to use SDK functions for developing interactive apps in the following chapters.

## 4.6. Classes, Objects and Inheritance in Swift

Classes and objects play an important role in "object-oriented" programming languages like Swift. Classes can be thought as template containers that have empty properties of the objects created using them. The relation of class and object concepts are as follows:

**1.** Firstly, a **class** that contains variables and functions is defined

**2.** This **class** definition is used to define **one or more objects**.

We can consider a car example to understand classes better. There are different cars having specific properties like colour, number of doors, brand, model year, etc. Car (as a concept) as can be considered as a class and each real car having specific properties can be thought as objects belonging to the car class. This is shown in Figure 4.33.

Let's create a car class in Swift as an example. Classes are defined similar to functions but without any parameters as in Code 4.41.

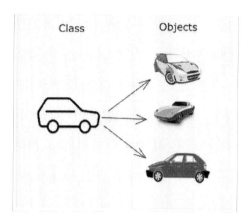

Figure 4.33. Class-object concept

```
class Car  {
    var colour: String

    init (colour: String) {
        self.colour = colour
    }
func askColour () -> String {
    return self.colour
    }
}
```
Code 4.41

This is a class definition example. This class has three main sections inside.

➢ First section is the definition of a variable called "colour". As you may have noticed, it isn't assigned a value since each instance of a "Car" object will have different colour property.

➢ The second section has a special function called **init**. It is used to set variables inside a class when creating an object. In this case, an object created using this class will have to be defined with a colour property and the **init** function will set the colour variable of the class to the passed colour data.

➢ Finally, this class has a function called "askColour". It returns the value of the colour variable when called.

Two objects named "myCar" and "yourCar" are created using the "Car" class below:

```
var myCar = Car(colour: "red")
var yourCar = Car(colour: "white")
```
Code 4.42

Please pay attention to object definitions. They are created similar to a variable however they are **instances** of the "Car" class. In the above code, "myCar" object is created having the red colour and the object named "yourCar" is created with white colour. Since there is a method in the class for asking their colour, **we can apply that method on these objects** to extract their respective colours:

```
print(myCar.askColour())
print(yourCar.askColour())
```
Code 4.43

Playground output of the class-object example is given in the following figure.

Figure 4.34. Class and object definitions in the playground

There's an important concept related to classes: **inheritance**. If a new class (class$_2$) inherits from an existing class (class$_1$), it means that class$_2$

65

takes variables and methods of class$_1$. As an example, let's define a new class inheriting from our existing Car class:

```
class hatchbackCar: Car {
    var length = "short"
}
```
Code 4.44

In the above code, the new class "hatchbackCar" **inherits** all the variables and methods of its **parent class** "Car". New classes inherit properties of a parent class with the following form: "class newClass: parentClass". Hence in the above code, "hatchbackCar" has the variable "colour" from its parent class while it additionally has the "length" variable. We can define a new object "myNewCar" from the new class and ask for its variables as in Code 4.45.

```
var myNewCar = hatchbackCar(colour: "black")
print(myNewCar.askColour())
print(myNewCar.length)
```
Code 4.45

The output of the playground is shown in the following figure:

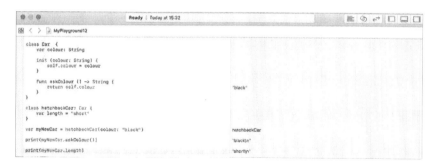

Figure 4.35. Printing the inherited and the specific properties of the new object

If you don't feel comfortable with classes, objects and inheritance for now, don't worry. You'll learn more about them when you use them in actual app development.

Well, I think this much of Swift basics is enough for starting to develop our iOS apps. Swift is, of course, a very extensive programming language and has much more to learn about it but this is a beginner's book and I think you're good to continue to app development.

The good news is that the boring stuff ends here and the fun stuff is beginning: developing apps that actually do something. In the next chapters, there will be a lot of hands on Swift coding which will make your apps to interact with the user such as changing screen colour by pushing a button and sending an SMS within your own app, etc. Let's get a coffee and relax for some time before continuing to the next chapter.

## Chapter 5

# iOS APP #1: DISCO LIGHTS

## 5.1. Creating the Project

We'll develop a **disco lights app** in our first Swift coded project. You'll see how we can interact with our app using a button and connecting this button to our code.

Our aim is to develop an app in which the screen background colour is changed in a disco light fashion. Each time we click a button, we want the background of the screen to take the following colours in a sequential order: red, orange, yellow, green, blue, cyan, purple and white.

Firstly, open Xcode and select "Create a new Xcode project" as shown in Figure 5.1. If your Xcode is already open, then select File → New → Project to create a new project.

Figure 5.1. Creating a new Xcode project

Since we'll just develop a single screen app, select the "Single View Application" in the dialog window shown in Figure 5.2. Click "Next" afterwards.

Figure 5.2. Selecting the single view app

Xcode will then ask for the main project parameters as in Figure 5.3. I named the project as "disco-lights" but you can give any name you want. On the other hand, you need to select a team as indicated by the arrow in the figure. If you cannot see an account to select, it means that you haven't set up code signing yet. In this case, please review Chapter 2 to set up code signing and continue after.

After naming your project and selecting the team, you're ready to save your project files, for that click "Next". In the next screen, Xcode just asks where to save the new project as shown in Figure 5.4. I selected my desktop but again you can select any place on your Mac to save.

## 5.2. Project Settings

After saving the project, Xcode opens it and shows the detailed project settings as in Figure 5.5. In this window, perhaps the most critical part is the so-called "Deployment info" section. The "deployment target" is the iOS version we'll develop our app for. Since we want to invest in the newest devices and technologies, it's better to develop for iOS 11, which Xcode 9 selects automatically as you can see in Figure 5.5. The other important setting is the "Devices" which is just below the iOS version box.

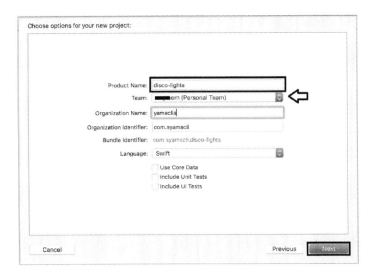

Figure 5.3. Basic project settings

The default is "Universal" and it's OK for us. It means that our app will run on all iOS devices having iOS 11 or later. In summary, there's no need to change anything in the detailed project settings window of Figure 5.5 for now.

We have reviewed the files that are automatically generated in an Xcode 9 project in Chapter 3. These files are shown in the left pane of the Xcode window as in Figure 5.6.

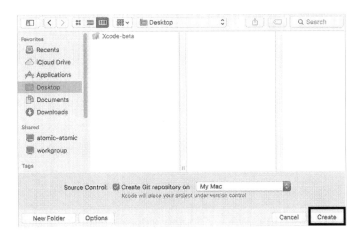

Figure 5.4. Saving your project files

Figure 5.5. Detailed project settings in Xcode 9

In this design, we will place a button in the middle of the device screen. When we click on it, the screen background will take the colours we listed before. In order to place a button on the screen, select the file "Main.storyboard" and the device screen will appear in the main Xcode window as shown in Figure 5.7. I selected the iPhone 8 screen size manually. If you want to select a different device, click on the "View as..." text at the bottom left and select the device. After selecting the device you want, click on the "View as..." text again to close the device selection menu.

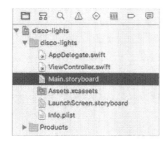

Figure 5.6. Files in our project

## 5.3. Adding a Button

We now have an empty screen. We need to place a button to click on. For this, find the "Button" component from the object library, then drag and drop it on the empty device screen as shown in Figure 5.8. If you try to place the button in the middle, Xcode will automatically show guiding lines in horizontal and vertical axes as shown in the figure, which helps you to drop the button component just in the middle. If you couldn't drop the button in the middle, don't worry. Xcode has advanced positioning methods. I'll now show you how to position it as you wish. Please see Figure 5.9 where I dropped the button somewhere in the screen and I now want to position it in the middle.

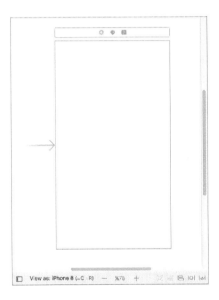

Figure 5.7. Main Xcode window showing the device screen

## 5.4. Adding Positioning Constraints

In Figure 5.9, I selected the button by single-clicking on it and then if I click on the two-rectangle shaped button shown by the arrow, I reach a popup menu where I can do some positioning operations regarding the selected component (button in this case). The popup menu is shown in Figure 5.10.

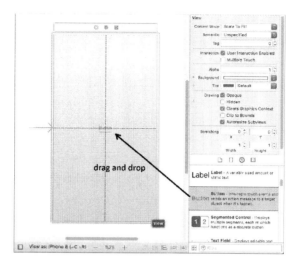

Figure 5.8. Placing a button component on the device screen

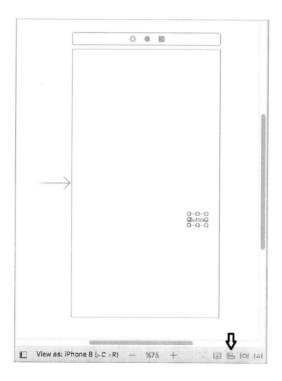

Figure 5.9. Positioning a component

We want to align our button horizontally and vertically on the screen (screen is the container here), therefore we need to tick the boxes to the left of the "Horizontally in Container" and "Vertically in Container" texts as shown inside the rectangle. After then, click on the "Add 2 Constraints" button (shown by the arrow in Figure 5.10) to add these constraints to our design. Our design now looks like Figure 5.11.

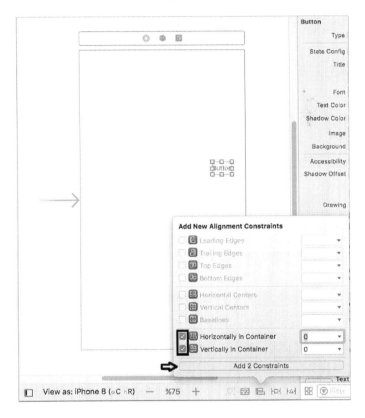

Figure 5.10. Alignment menu

The added constraints now appear in the design tree as shown in the rectangular box in Figure 5.11. However, the button position didn't change yet. For viewing the results of the newly added constraints, press the button shown inside the rectangle in Figure 5.12 to update frames.

After you update frames, your screen should look like Figure 5.13 i.e. the button should be positioned in the middle of the screen. If not, try the steps above again to make sure you applied all the steps correctly.

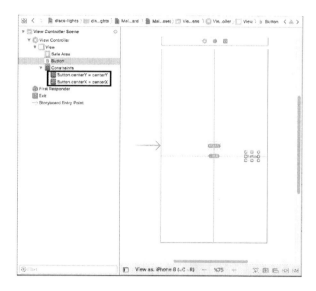

Figure 5.11. Our design after adding constraints

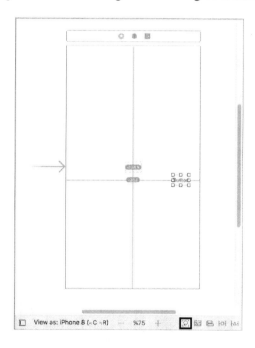

Figure 5.12. Updating frames

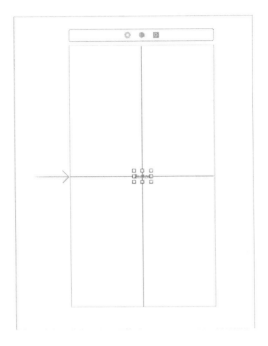

Figure 5.13. Device screen after updating frames

## 5.5. Editing Button Attributes

Now, let's change some properties of the button component. For this, select it by a single-click and then press the "Show attributes inspector" button as shown inside the rectangle in Figure 5.14.

I'll change the text of the button from "Button" to "Change!" in the box shown by the arrow in Figure 5.14. I'll also change the font size to 20 from the menu shown by the ellipse in the figure. After these changes, the user interface looks like Figure 5.15. Note that you may need to drag the edges of the button if you cannot see the text "Change!" at full length.

## 5.6. Connecting Button to the Code

We're now ready to write our code in Swift. In order to connect the button (or any component that may exist in our user interface) to our code, we need to open the "Assistant editor" of Xcode. To do this, select the double-circle as shown inside the box in Figure 5.16. Note that this button group lies at the top right of the main Xcode window.

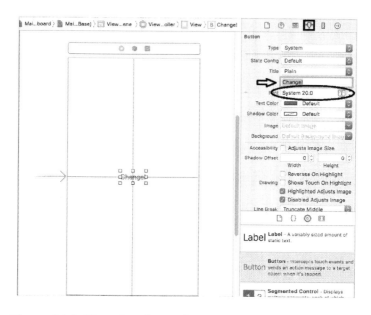

Figure 5.14. Changing the attributes of the button component

Figure 5.15. Finalized screen setup

Figure 5.16. Switching to the "Assistant editor"

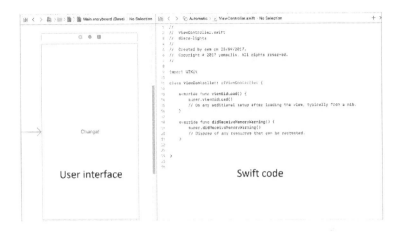

User interface | Swift code

Figure 5.17. Assistant editor

When the assistant editor opens, the Xcode main screen looks as in Figure 5.17. Xcode shows the user interface (screen) and the Swift code related to this screen together. It is useful to check what's already there in the Swift code. The code automatically generated by Xcode is shown in Code 5.1. In this code, the first line imports the user interface kit, which is needed for all user interface functions. And then a class definition comes: **class ViewController: UIViewController**.The "ViewController" class is the main class of our user interface. As you can see, it inherits the methods and variables of the class "UIViewController". And then two methods are generated: **viewDidLoad()** and **didReceiveMemoryWarning()**. These are general methods that check the proper loading and the memory problems related to the user interface.

```
import UIKit
class ViewController: UIViewController {
    override func viewDidLoad() {
        super.viewDidLoad()
        }
    override func didReceiveMemoryWarning() {
        super.didReceiveMemoryWarning()
    }
}
```
Code 5.1

Whatever we'll design will execute inside the main class: "ViewController". We need to keep this in mind.

The "ViewController" class is the main class however it doesn't know about the components placed on the user interface until we tell. **We need to connect the components of the user interface (the button in this example) to the code.** In order to do this, Xcode offers an easy method. Just single-click on the button and select it. Then, hold down the Ctrl key on the keyboard and drag the button to the Swift code as shown in Figure 5.18. Xcode will show a connection line. You can drop the line anywhere in the main class. When you drop it (i.e., stop clicking the left mouse button and release the Ctrl key), Xcode will ask you about the connection you want to make. This dialog box is shown in Figure 5.19. In this dialog box, the connection type is important. "Outlet" type is used for static components such as a text label while the "Action" type is used for components that cause an action in your app. In our example, the button will trigger the colour changes hence it will cause an action. Thus, we'll select the "Action" type for the connection as shown in Figure 5.19.

Then we need to type a name for the connection. It can be anything you want but it's of course a good practice to give a meaningful name. I named it as "changeColours". After setting the connection's type and name, click "connect" in this dialog box and then the connection will be completed. The connection appears as an @IBAction function in Swift code as shown inside the rectangle box in Figure 5.20. This function is also shown in Code 5.2.

```
@IBAction func changeColours(_ sender: Any) {
    }
```
Code 5.2

## 5.7. Writing the Swift Code of the App

We'll write button's actions inside its function shown in Code 5.2. We want the screen background colour to take the mentioned colours in a sequence but for now, let's start with a simple code that will show if our button and the connection work properly. Let's change the screen background colour to red when the button is clicked. In order to do user interface related actions in Xcode and Swift, we will use the **self** keyword, which refers to the current view.

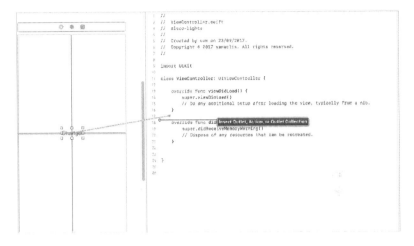

Figure 5.18. Connecting the user interface to the code

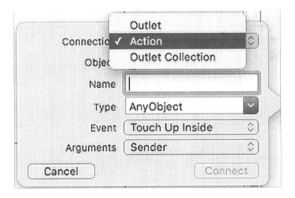

Figure 5.19. Xcode dialog for connection

Figure 5.20. The established connection in the code

We will change the current screen's (self's) view's (its appearance) background colour to the user interface colour of red. Let's translate this statement to Swift language:

```
self.view.backgroundColor = UIColor.red
```
Code 5.3

This code changes the background colour to red. We'll insert this code in the button's **@IBAction** function and then the whole ViewController.swift code should look like below:

```
import UIKit
class ViewController: UIViewController {
    override func viewDidLoad() {
        super.viewDidLoad()
        }
    @IBAction func changeColours(_ sender: Any) {
        self.view.backgroundColor = UIColor.red
    }
    override func didReceiveMemoryWarning() {
        super.didReceiveMemoryWarning()
            }
}
```
Code 5.4

Let's run our app in the simulator. For that please press the "Run" button at the top of Xcode (as explained in Chapter 3, Figure 3.11). After then, the simulator will start with our app loaded as shown in Figure 5.21.

Figure 5.21. User interface of our app when it first starts

Now, it's the great moment. Click on the "Change!" button and hopefully the screen background colour will change to red as shown in Figure 5.22. Note that clicking the button again will have no effect since the background is red and the code we have written inside the button's **IBAction** won't do anything different. Let's improve our code so that it will change the background colour to red, orange, yellow, green, blue, cyan, purple and then white again as we click on the button.

There are various ways to do this but I'll define an array which holds the colour values that the background colour will take as follows:

```
let colours: [UIColor] = [UIColor.red, UIColor.orange,
UIColor.yellow, UIColor.green, UIColor.cyan,
UIColor.blue, UIColor.white]
```
Code 5.5

Figure 5.22. Background colour changes to red after clicking the button (full resolution colour figures online at: www.yamaclis.com/ios11)

The type of the elements of this array is **UIColor** as you can see. The reason of defining this array is that we can easily sweep the array elements as we click on the "Change!" button. We can modify button's **IBAction** function as in Code 5.6 that will change the background colour by taking elements from the **colours** array.

```
var i = 0
@IBAction func changeColours(_ sender: Any){
        self.view.backgroundColor = colours[i]
        i += 1
        if ( i == colours.count ) {
            i = 0
        }
    }
```
Code 5.6

Here is the explanation of this code:

➤   The line **self.view.backgroundColor = colours[i]** changes the background colour according to current array element **colours[i]**.
➤   Note the variable declaration before the button code. This variable, "i", holds the array index and initialized to 0. Hence at the start, **colours [i] = colours [0] =UIColor.red**.

➤ Each time the button is pressed, this index variable is incremented by 1 with the code **i += 1**.

➤ However, we have a problem. The **colours** array has 7 elements. Remember that the array index starts with 0 hence the elements of the **colours** array have the following indices: 0, 1, 2, 3, 4, 5, 6. When we click the button for 7 times, then the variable **i** will have the value of 7 and our app will crash since the expression **colours[7]** is invalid, it can take the values up to **colours[6]**.

➤ In order to prevent this, we have added an **if** statement that checks if the index variable reaches the element count of the **colours** array: **if ( i == colours.count ) {i = 0}**. (The expression **colours.count** returns the number of elements of the **colours** array, 7 for our case). If the index variable **i** reaches the number of array elements, it is reset to 0.

➤ In short: when the variable **i** reaches the maximum value it can take, it is reset to 0 so that we can start sweeping the colours array from the beginning.

The complete code of the ViewController.swift file is shown below:

```
import UIKit
class ViewController: UIViewController {
    let colours: [UIColor] = [UIColor.red,
        UIColor.orange, UIColor.yellow, UIColor.green,
        UIColor.cyan, UIColor.blue, UIColor.white]
    var i = 0
    override func viewDidLoad() {
        super.viewDidLoad()
        }
    @IBAction func changeColours(_ sender: Any) {
        self.view.backgroundColor = colours[i]
        i += 1
        if ( i >= colours.count ) {
            i = 0
        }
    }
    override func didReceiveMemoryWarning() {
        super.didReceiveMemoryWarning()
}
}
```

Code 5.7

## 5.8. Building and Running the App

Let's run our disco-lights app. Run the project in a simulator and click on the "Change!" button a lot of times. The screen should take the colours of red, orange, yellow, green, cyan, blue, white, red, orange, yellow, green, cyan, blue, white, red, orange, yellow, green, cyan, blue, white, red, orange, yellow, green, cyan, blue, white, red, orange, yellow, green, cyan, blue, white, red, orange, yellow, green, cyan, blue, white etc. **Sorry, just checking white, red, orange, yellow, green, cyan, blue, white is enough...** I have shown different colours I obtained as I clicked the "Change!" button in Figure 5.23.

You can install this app on your real device as explained in the last pages of Chapter 3. I verified that this app runs on real devices (iPhone SE, iPad Mini and iPad Air 2) as expected. You can of course install and run this app on any iOS device.

Figure 5.23. Different screen colours obtained as the " Change!" button is clicked (colour figure on the book's website: www.yamaclis.com/ios11)

# Chapter 6

# iOS APP # 2: BODY MASS INDEX CALCULATOR

## 6.1. General Information

Body mass index (BMI) is a figure of merit that is used for assessing the thickness-thinness of a person. BMI is defined as the ratio of the mass and height-squared with the formula below:

$$BMI = \frac{mass\,(kg)}{(height\,(m))^2}$$

After the calculation of the BMI, the following table is the used for assessing the weight category:

| Weight category | from BMI | to BMI |
|---|---|---|
| Very severely underweight | 0 | 15 |
| Severely underweight | 15 | 16 |
| Underweight | 16 | 18.5 |
| Normal (healthy weight) | 18.5 | 25 |
| Overweight | 25 | 30 |
| Obese Class I (Moderately obese) | 30 | 35 |
| Obese Class II (Severely obese) | 35 | 40 |
| Obese Class III (Very severely obese) | 40 | - |

Table 6.1. Weight categories
(source: https://en.wikipedia.org/wiki/Body_mass_index)

In this chapter, we'll develop a BMI calculator app and learn to use user inputs, make calculations inside our code and display results to the user.

In order to calculate the BMI in our app, we obviously need weight and height inputs. Our Swift code will calculate the BMI using the formula above and then it will decide the category according to Table 6.1. First of all, let's create the user interface of our app. In Xcode, create a new project called "BMI Calculator" and save it anywhere you want on your Mac. (I'll not repeat myself about these things, these were explained in detail in the previous chapters).

Firstly, let's place a UI component called "Label" to the user interface as shown in Figure 6.1. "Label" is a static text, the user cannot edit it but the app can change the text written in the Label. Please place the label in the middle of the screen with the help of the guiding lines as we did in the previous chapter. After placing the "Label", please select it and then change its text to "BMI Calculator" as shown by the upper arrow in Figure 6.1. Drag the edge of the label box to fit the text inside as we did before. **I have placed numbers in Figure 6.1 to indicate the order of the operations.**

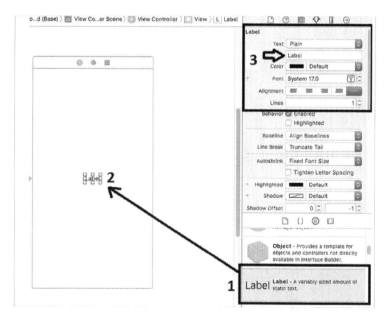

Figure 6.1. Adding a "Label" component

## 6.2. Adding and Positioning the Labels

After editing the text, select the label component and align it in horizontal and vertical axes as shown in Figure 6.2: tick the boxes shown and then click "Add Constraints".

Figure 6.2. Aligning the label component horizontally and vertically

Now, the label should be aligned in the middle of the screen as follows:

Figure 6.3. The Label in the middle of the screen

We'll place other components on the screen so we don't need the title "BMI Calculator" to lie in the middle vertically. Therefore, we'll move it up a bit. To do this, select the y-constraint (1) as shown in Figure 6.4, which will display the constraints attributes section (2).

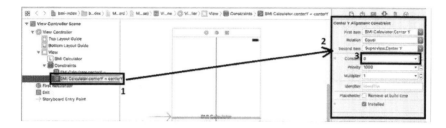

Figure 6.4. Selecting the y-axis constraints

Change the "Constant" value (shown by (3) in Figure 6.4) from 0 to -200 and then hit return on the keyboard. The "BMI Calculator" label will move up 200 units as shown in Figure 6.5.

Similarly, we will place four more label components as shown in Figure 6.6. These are labels for: weight, height, BMI and the category.

Figure 6.5. The label component at its desired place
(200 units above the vertical middle)

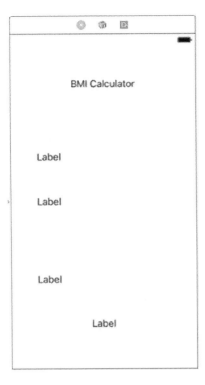

Figure 6.6. Adding four more labels to the user interface

We can now change the texts of these labels as: "Enter your weight (kg):", "Enter your height (m):", "Your BMI result:", "Category appears here!" as shown in Figure 6.7.

Alignment plays a central role in app design as we explained before. We need to align the objects in the user interface so that they will appear as expected for different screen sizes. Until now, we only aligned the title label "BMI Calculator". We need to align the new 4 labels too. However, instead of aligning them with horizontal and vertical guide lines, it is more practical to align them relative to each other. In other words, we'll first align "Enter your weight" label relative to the "BMI Calculator" label. And then we'll position the next label "Enter your height" relative to the "Enter your weight" label and so on. Let's align the "Enter your weight" label relative to the "BMI Calculator" label. First, select the "Enter your weight" label and then click on the "Pin" button shown inside the small rectangle in Figure 6.8.

Figure 6.7. Label texts in the user interface

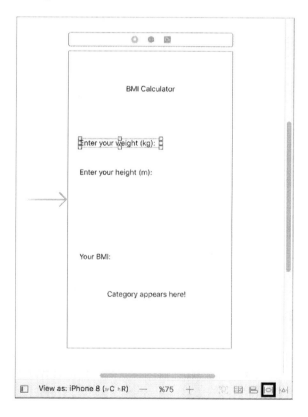

Figure 6.8. Selecting the "Pin" menu

The "Pin" menu enables us to set various parameters of the selected component such as width and height as shown in Figure 6.9. There are also settings for the "Spacing to the nearest neighbour" shown inside the big rectangle in Figure 6.9. This part will help us position the components relative to each other or relative to the edges.

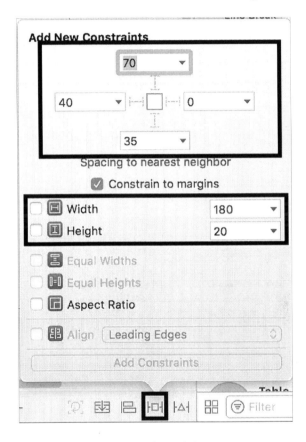

Figure 6.9. The "Pin" menu

It is worth noting that Xcode asks us to provide both height, width, and 2 spacing constraints to complete the positioning of the label, if there's a missing constraint then Xcode won't update the frame.

We can specify the width and height values of the "Enter your weight" label as 180 and 20  respectively as shown in the dialog box in Figure 6.10 (of course you can use any value as long as the text fits inside). Then, we'll specify its distance to the "nearest neighbour above" as 70 units. We can also specify its distance to the device's left edge as 5 units. The spacing section looks as shown below with these values:

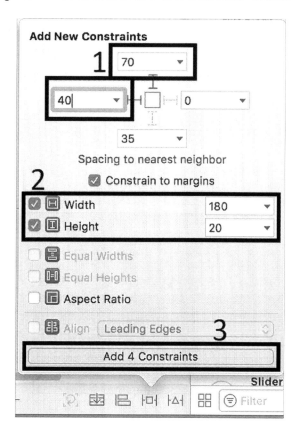

Figure 6.10. Setting the constraints of "Enter your weight" label

These four constraints are enough to represent the dimensions and the spacing of this label. After you clicking on "Add 4 Constraints" button, you can see that these constraints are now included in the scene explorer as in Figure 6.11.

After you add these constraints, your screen should look like Figure 6.12. It is good to summarize what we did up to here using Figure 6.12: We set the fixed position constraints of the "BMI Calculator" label (shown by rectangle 1) and then we set the relative constraints of the "Enter your weight" label (shown by rectangle 2). We still need to position remaining three labels shown inside ellipses in Figure 6.12.

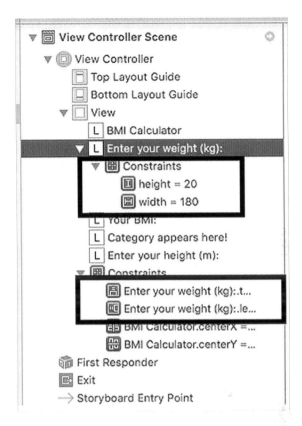

Figure 6.11. Newly added constraints shown in the scene explorer

It is worth noting that we also need to add text fields (boxes that we can input text) to enter the weight and height values and for displaying the BMI result. In addition, we have to include a button to calculate the BMI. The textboxes to enter the weight and the height will be next to their labels and the BMI result textbox will be next to the "Your BMI:" label. I'll put the "Calculate" button between the "Enter your weight" section and the "Your BMI" section but note that these are only personal choices, you can position your components as you wish and it'll be true as long as the components do not overlap. Anyway, let's align the "Enter your height", "Your BMI" and "Category" labels using the positioning and width/height values shown in Figures 6.13, 6.14 and 6.15, respectively.

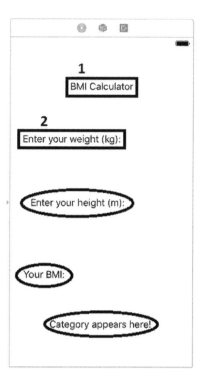

Figure 6.12. Device screen after updating frames

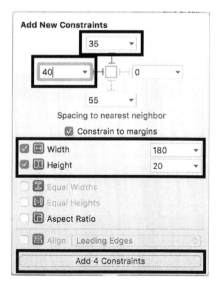

Figure 6.13. Constraints for the "Enter your height" label

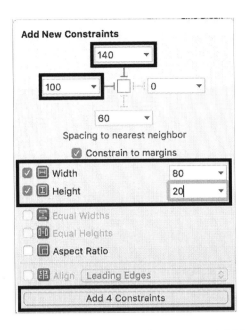

Figure 6.14. Constraints for the "Your BMI" label

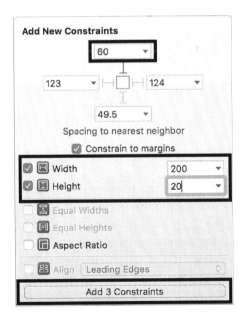

Figure 6.15. Constraints for the "Category" label

Note that, there are 3 constraints set from the "Pin" menu for the "Category" label in Figure 6.15. Since it won't have any other component next to it (since it'll show words like "normal" which is the result), I decided to align it in the middle horizontally. I did it from the "Alignment" menu as in Figure 6.16 (we did it before, you may remember). After updating frames, we obtain the device screen shown in Figure 6.17.

## 6.3. Adding the Text Fields and the Button

We'll now place "text fields" that will enable us to input the weight and height information. Text fields can also be used for displaying text hence we'll use it also for displaying the calculated BMI next to the label "Your BMI:". In the component menu of Xcode, just search for "text" and then drag and drop three "Text Fields": next to the weight (1), height (2) and BMI labels (3) as shown in as shown in Figure 6.18.

Figure 6.16. Horizontal alignment of the "Category" label

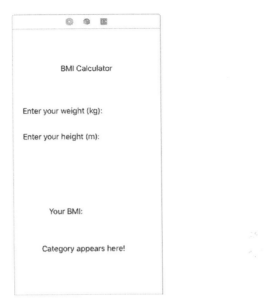

Figure 6.17. Final view of the label components in our screen

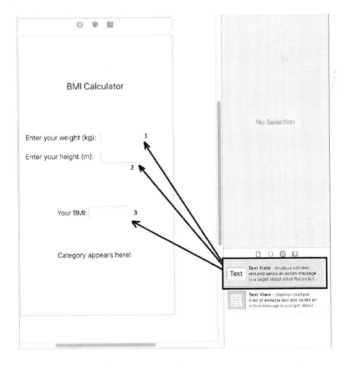

Figure 6.18. Adding text fields to the user interface

Finally, let's insert the button that will trigger the BMI calculation in between the height input and BMI output sections as shown in Figure 6.19. And then we will proceed for the final touches to position the newly added components.

We are now ready to set the positions of the new components on the device screen:

➢ Text field of weight: Select the text field next to the weight label. Then, using the "Pin" menu, set the constraints of its position and size as in Figure 6.20. **Make sure that the "Enter your weight" label is selected as the relative element for the left constraint as shown in Figure 6.20.**

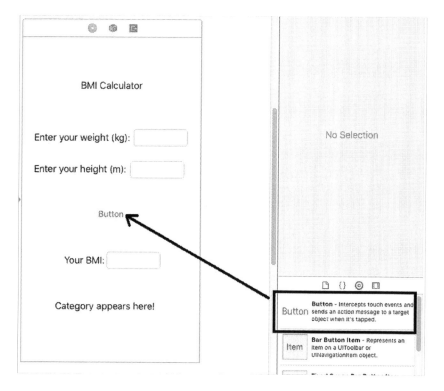

Figure 6.19. Adding the last component: the button

➢ Text field of height: We set constraints of this text field as shown in Figure 6.21. Note that our aim is to position this text box next to the height label.

➢ Button: I have increased the font size of the button to 25 and also changed its text to "Calculate my BMI!". The constraints for this button are given in Figure 6.22.

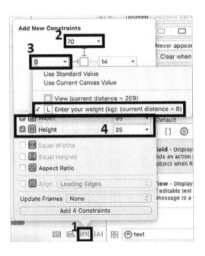

Figure 6.20. Adding constraints for the weight input text field

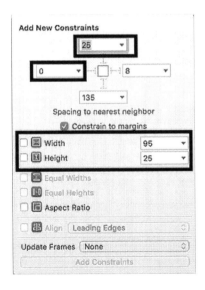

Figure 6.21. Constraints for the height input text field

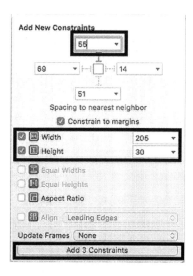

Figure 6.22. Constraints for the button

Note that we have added only three constraints here because it'd be better to align it horizontally with the "Align" menu as shown in Figure 6.23.

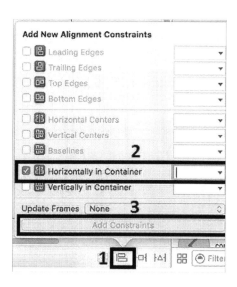

Figure 6.23. Aligning the button horizontally in the container

➤ Your BMI label: The following constraints are appropriate for this component:

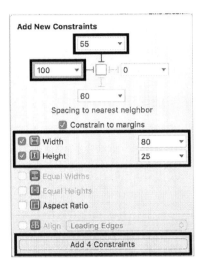

Figure 6.24. Constraints for the "Your BMI" label

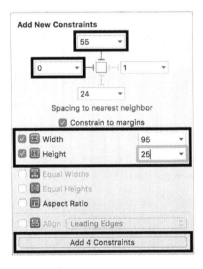

Figure 6.25. Constraints for the BMI display text field

> BMI text field: Since this component is supposed to be next to the "Your BMI" label, the settings shown in Figure 6.25 do the job.

> The category label: We'll add three constraints for that and then align it horizontally similar to the one we did for the button. The constraints for the category label are as in Figure 6.26 while its horizontal positioning can be made as shown before in Figure 6.23.

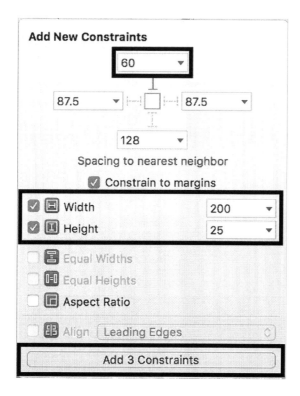

Figure 6.26. Adding constraints for the "Category" label

Before moving on to writing the code for our app, I changed the colours of the title and the category labels. You can also change their properties as you like. In addition, since I'll not enter any value into the BMI text field but only read the value calculated by the app, I made this text field disabled for text inputs. For this, select this text field and then deselect the "user interaction enabled" box as shown in Figure 6.27 from the right pane of Xcode.

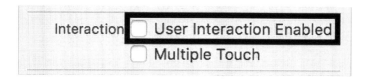

Figure 6.27. The user interaction option in Xcode

After these alignments and editing operations, the user interface looks like Figure 6.28.

Figure 6.28. The appearance of the user interface

## 6.4. Connecting the Objects to the Code

As we did in the previous app, we'll now connect the interactive elements to the Swift code. Weight, height and BMI text fields, the "Calculate my BMI!" button and the "Category appears here!" labels are interactive, they'll either provide input to the calculation or they'll display the results of the calculation. **We'll set the connection type of the "Calculate my BMI!" button as an IBAction and all other elements as IBOutlets.** After these connections, the ViewController.swift file will look like below:

```
import UIKit
class ViewController: UIViewController {

        override func viewDidLoad() {
        super.viewDidLoad()
```

```
        // Do any additional setup after loading the
view, typically from a nib.
    }
    @IBOutlet weak var weightInput: UITextField!
    @IBOutlet weak var heightInput: UITextField!
    @IBOutlet weak var BMIOutput: UITextField!
    @IBOutlet weak var categoryOutput: UILabel!
    @IBAction func calcBMI(_ sender: Any) {
    }
    override func didReceiveMemoryWarning() {
        super.didReceiveMemoryWarning()
        // Dispose of any resources that can be
recreated.
    }
}
```

Code 6.1 (cont'd from the previous page)

## 6.5. Developing the Main Code of the App

We'll pull the values entered in the weight and height text input boxes, perform the BMI calculation according to the equation given before, show the resulting BMI value in the BMI text field and then check the BMI category according to the BMI table using switch-case statements.

**1.** Firstly, let's read the weight and height values from the text fields. It's better to take these values when the button is pressed therefore we'll write this code inside the button's function **@IBAction func calcBMI(_ sender: Any)** as in Code 6.2.

```
@IBAction func calcBMI(_ sender: Any) {
if let heightStr = heightInput.text {
 if heightStr == "" {
   return
 }
 else {
   if let weightStr = weightInput.text {
     if weightStr == "" {
       return
     }
     else {
         if let heightNum = Double(heightStr)  {
         if let weightNum = Double(weightStr)  {
                     } }
             }
}}
```

Code 6.2

As you can see from Code 6.2, the string entered in the weight and height text fields are taken by the **heightInput.text** and **weightInput.text** structures: **if let heightStr = heightInput.text** and **if let weightStr = weightInput.text** statements assign the text inputs to the **heightStr** and **weightStr** constants. The nested if-else structures are used to control if values are actually entered in these text fields by checking **if heightStr == ""** and **if weightStr == ""** conditions. If any of these conditions is true (meaning that nothing is entered in one or both text fields), a **return** statement is executed and the program exits doing nothing other. In the end, **if let heightNum = Double(heightStr)** and **if let weightNum = Double(weightStr)** statements are used to convert the string values of **heightStr** and **weightStr** to Double type and then assign them to **heightNum** and **weightNum** variables. The **if** statements are used here since we're not sure if the texts entered into height and weight fields can be converted to Double type (the user may enter a non-numerical text and that cannot be converted to Double type). **If these texts are convertible to Double type then we will have the numerical values of height and weight stored in heightNum and weightNum constants.**

**2.** The BMI is calculated according to the equation given in the beginning of this chapter using the code shown in Code 6.3. Note that a constant named BMI is created and then the result of the calculation is assigned to it in the first line. In the second line, numerical BMI is converted to String type and it is assigned to the text of the BMIOutput label.

```
let BMI: Double = (weightNum) / (heightNum * heightNum)
BMIOutput.text = String(BMI)
```
Code 6.3

**3.** Finally, the switch-case statements are employed to check the calculated BMI value according to Table 6.1 as in Code 6.4. In each of the cases, the text of the **categoryOutput** is set accordingly.

```
switch BMI {
    case 1..<15:
      categoryOutput.text = "Very severely underweight"
    case 15...16:
      categoryOutput.text = "Severely underweight"
    case 16..<18.5:
      categoryOutput.text = "Underweight"
    case 18.5...<25:
      categoryOutput.text = "Normal"
    case 25..<30:
      categoryOutput.text = "Overweight"
    case 30..<35:
      categoryOutput.text = "Moderately obese"
    case 35..<40:
      categoryOutput.text = "Severely obese"
    case 40..<60:
      categoryOutput.text = "Very severely obese"
    default:
      return
}
```
Code 6.4 (cont'd from the previous page)

Combining all of these codes, the complete ViewController.swift file of our app is obtained as the following (**you can download these codes from the book's website:** www.yamaclis.com/ios11):

```
import UIKit

class ViewController: UIViewController {
```

```swift
            @IBOutlet weak var weightInput: UITextField!
            @IBOutlet weak var heightInput: UITextField!
            @IBOutlet weak var BMIOutput: UITextField!
            @IBOutlet weak var categoryOutput: UILabel!

            override func viewDidLoad() {
            super.viewDidLoad()
            // Do any additional setup after loading the
view, typically from a nib.

    }

            @IBAction func calcBMI(_ sender: Any) {
            if let heightStr = heightInput.text {
                if heightStr == "" {
                return
                }
                else {
                    if let weightStr = weightInput.text {
                        if weightStr == "" {
                            return
                        }
                        else {
if let heightNum = Double(heightStr) {
if let weightNum = Double(weightStr) {
let BMI: Double = (weightNum) / (heightNum * heightNum)
BMIOutput.text = String(BMI)

switch BMI {
 case 1..<15:
   categoryOutput.text = "Very severely underweight"
 case 15...16:
   categoryOutput.text = "Severely underweight"
 case 16..<18.5:
   categoryOutput.text = "Underweight"
 case 18.5..<25:
   categoryOutput.text = "Normal"
 case 25..<30:
   categoryOutput.text = "Overweight"
 case 30..<35:
   categoryOutput.text = "Moderately obese"
 case 35..<40:
   categoryOutput.text = "Severely obese"
 case 40..<60:
   categoryOutput.text = "Very severely obese"
 default:
```

```
    return
                                 }
                         }
                    }
                }
            }
        }
    }
}
    override func didReceiveMemoryWarning() {
        super.didReceiveMemoryWarning()
        // Dispose of any resources that can be
recreated.
    }
}
```

Code 6.5 (cont'd from the previous pages)

## 6.6. Building and Running the App

Let's now try our app in the simulator. Just hit the "Run" button while the iPhone 8 simulator is selected and you should see the user interface shown in Figure 6.29.

Enter weight and height values (in kg and metres) and then tap the "Calculate my BMI!" button. If you followed all steps correctly, you should see the BMI value and the BMI category on your app screen as in Figure 6.30.

## 6.7. Final Notes

**Note 1.** You can set the keyboard type that will pop up on a real device while entering the height and weight values by selecting the respective text field and then setting the "keyboard type" from "Text Input Traits" section of the attributes menu in Xcode as shown in Figure 6.31. It's better to select "Numbers and punctuation" in our app since we don't want the user to enter any text.

Figure 6.29. The user interface of the BMI calculator app

**Note 2.** The text field that shows the BMI index cannot accommodate the all the digits as you can see from Figure 6.30. You can either increase the width of the text field or set the text with `BMIOutput.text = String(Int(BMI))` which will just show the integer part of the BMI.

Figure 6.30. Our BMI calculator app in action

**Note 3.** In the simulator, the keyboard may not show up by default. In order to switch the keyboard, you can select/deselect Hardware → Keyboard → Connect Hardware Keyboard from the Simulator menu while the simulator is the active window.

Figure 6.31. Changing the popup keyboard type

**Note 4.** I have verified that the BMI calculator app runs on real devices as expected (installing on a real device was explained in the last pages of Chapter 3). However, there's a problem with devices having moderate screens. After entering height and weight info, the keyboard does not disappear and the user cannot click on the button and see her/his BMI result. In order to make the keyboard disappear after clicking on the "Return" key, you can use a method called **textFieldShouldReturn**. In order to use this method, we need to add the **UITextFieldDelegate** class to extend our ViewController class. We can use this method as shown in Code 6.6.

```
func textFieldShouldReturn(_ textField: UITextField) -
> Bool {
        self.weightInput.resignFirstResponder()
        self.heightInput.resignFirstResponder()
        return true
}
```
Code 6.6

When the user enters the height and weight info and taps the "Return" key on the real device, this method is called and it makes the keyboard to disappear. The whole ViewController.swift file with this method and its class added is shown below:

```
import UIKit

class ViewController: UIViewController, UITextFieldDelega
te {

        @IBOutlet weak var weightInput: UITextField!
        @IBOutlet weak var heightInput: UITextField!
        @IBOutlet weak var BMIOutput: UITextField!
        @IBOutlet weak var categoryOutput: UILabel!

        override func viewDidLoad() {
        super.viewDidLoad()
            self.weightInput.delegate = self
            self.heightInput.delegate = self
    }
@IBAction func calcBMI(_ sender: Any) {
        if let heightStr = heightInput.text {
            if heightStr == "" {
                return
            }
        else {
          if let weightStr = weightInput.text {
          if weightStr == "" {
          return
          }
          else {
if let heightNum = Double(heightStr) {
 if let weightNum = Double(weightStr) {
   let BMI: Double = (weightNum) / (heightNum *heightNum)
   BMIOutput.text = String(BMI)
    switch BMI {
      case 1..<15:
        categoryOutput.text = "Very severely underweight"
      case 15...16:
        categoryOutput.text = "Severely underweight"
      case 16..<18.5:
        categoryOutput.text = "Underweight"
      case 18.5..<25:
       categoryOutput.text = "Normal"
      case 25..<30:
```

```
                categoryOutput.text = "Overweight"
            case 30..<35:
                categoryOutput.text = "Moderately obese"
            case 35..<40:
                categoryOutput.text = "Severely obese"
            case 40..<60:
                categoryOutput.text = "Very severely obese"
            default:
                return
                                }
                            }
                        }
                    }
                }
            }
        }
    }
    func textFieldShouldReturn(_ textField: UITextField) -
> Bool {
            self.weightInput.resignFirstResponder()
            self.heightInput.resignFirstResponder()
            return true
        }

    override func didReceiveMemoryWarning() {
        super.didReceiveMemoryWarning()
        // Dispose of any resources that can be
recreated.
        }
}
```

Code 6.7 (cont'd from the previous page)

**Note 5.** Don't worry if the app categorizes you obese, it does me too (the values shown in Figure 6.30 are not mine ☺). I'm trying to do exercises and eat food with lower calories to decrease my BMI. (Sorry, this monologue made me hungry. See you in the next chapter later after having a big meal!).

# Chapter 7

## iOS APP # 3: SIMPLE DIE ROLLER

### 7.1. Creating the Project and Adding an Image View Object

In this chapter we will develop a die rolling app. We'll learn how to use images in the user interface and also the basic random number generation procedure in Swift. When we hit a rolling button, the app will choose a number between 1 and 6 randomly, show the result as a number in a label and also display a die image showing the outcome.

Please create a new project and save it on your computer. First of all, let's design the user interface. We need an image view component which is used to display an image or an animation of images. While the Main.storyboard file is selected in Xcode, find the Image View object in the object library and add it by drag and drop operation somewhere in the user interface as shown in Figure 7.1.

Let's align the image view on the screen and set its height and width values. Select the image view with a single-click, and then check the horizontal and vertical alignment in the "Align" menu. We'll add a button and a label below the image view therefore it is better to position the image view a bit above the vertical centre. For that, set the vertical alignment value to -100 as shown in Figure 7.2.

Since we'll show a die face in this image view, it's better to have a square shape. In order to set the height and width values of the image view, single-click to select it and then in the "Pin" menu set the height and width values you like. I set them to 128 as in Figure 7.3. After the position and dimension settings, image view appears on the Main.storyboard file as shown in Figure 7.4.

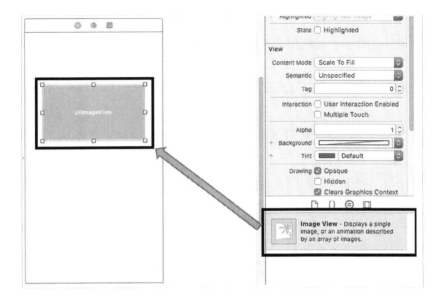

Figure 7.1. Adding an image view

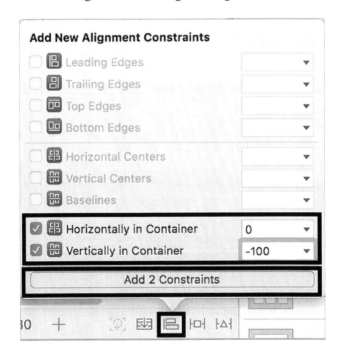

Figure 7.2. Adding alignment constraints for the image view

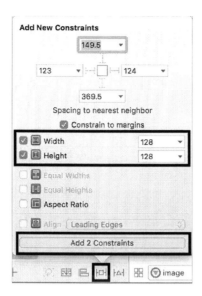

Figure 7.3. Setting the dimensions of the image view

Figure 7.4. Image view after the position and dimension settings

Now, we shall add a label component to show the outcome of the die roll as a text. Find the label component from the object library and then drag and drop to add it somewhere below the image view in the device screen as shown in Figure 7.5. This label will show the outcome as a number but before the rolling, it may show any default text you can set in the label text box shown by the ellipse in Figure 7.5. I set it as "Waiting...". I also set the text alignment as centred.

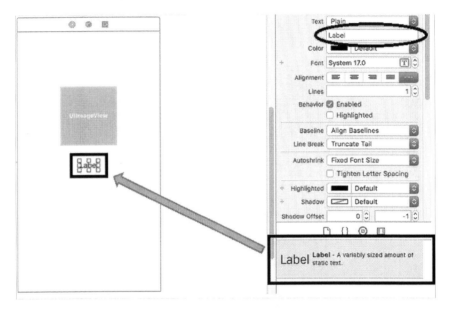

Figure 7.5. Adding a label component to show the rolling outcome as a number

Let's set the position and size constraints for the label component. I set the height and width to 25 and 128, respectively as shown in Figure 7.6.

The positioning constraints of the label will be set as "align horizontally in the container" from the "Align" menu as given in Figure 7.7 and 50 units below the nearest component above it with the "Pin" menu as shown in Figure 7.8.

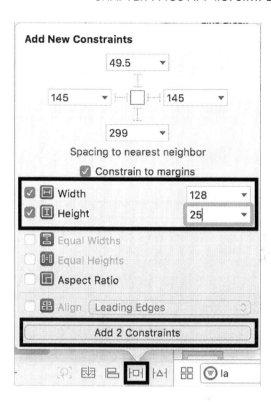

Figure 7.6. Width and height constraints for the label

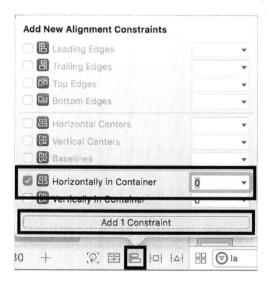

Figure 7.7. Alignment of the label horizontally

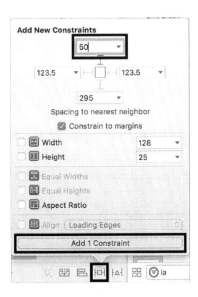

Figure 7.8. Setting the vertical constraint for the label

After these constraints, we have the label positioned 50 units below the image view component and aligned in the middle horizontally as shown below:

Figure 7.9. Image view and label components after alignment

Finally we need to add a button which will perform the die roll. Find the button component from the object library and drag and drop it somewhere below the label component as shown in Figure 7.10. After adding the button, you can set its text to something related to what it will do. I set its text to "Roll!" and changed its font size to 25.

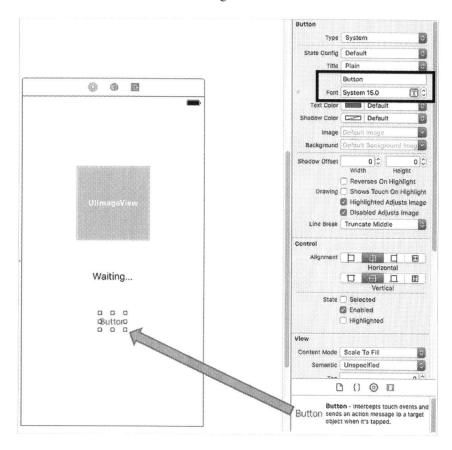

Figure 7.10. Adding the button

Now it's time for setting its dimension and alignment constraints. From the "Pin" menu, I set its height to 30, height to 80 and its distance to the component above it (the label) to 50 units as shown in Figure 7.11.

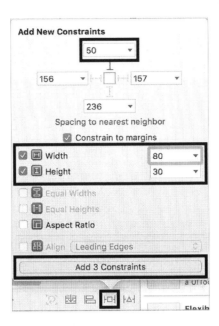

Figure 7.11. Adding height, width and vertical constraints of the button

After aligning its horizontal position to the middle from the "Align" menu as shown in Figure 7.12, we are ready to update the frame as in Figure 7.13. Remember that these buttons are located at the bottom right of the middle pane of Xcode.

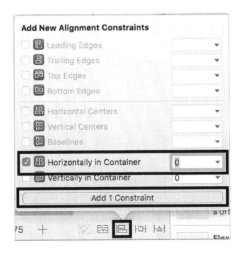

Figure 7.12. Setting the horizontal alignment of the button

"Update Frames" button

Figure 7.13. Updating frames in the user interface

After updating frames, the user interface should look like Figure 7.14. This is not the best user interface I know, but it'll do the job. You can do more artwork on it if you wish.

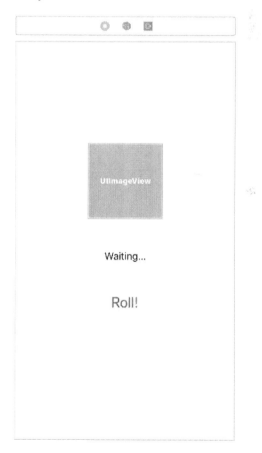

Figure 7.14. Final view of the device screen

## 7.2. Adding Images to the Project

We want to generate a random number in the range of 1 to 6 and then show the corresponding die image in the UIImageView object. Therefore we need the images of die faces from 1 to 6. I downloaded royalty-free die face images from the Internet and you can access them from this book's website www.yamaclis.com/ios11. These images are shown in Figure 7.15 together with their filenames.

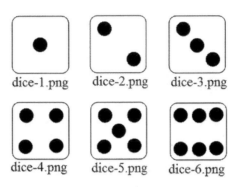

dice-1.png    dice-2.png    dice-3.png

dice-4.png    dice-5.png    dice-6.png

Figure 7.15. Die face images used in our app

As explained in Chapter 2, the file Assets.xcassets stores the images and similar data files that are used in the app. We open this file by single-clicking it inside the Xcode and then we are presented with an empty file as shown in Figure 7.16.

Figure 7.16. Empty "assets file"

In order to add images, right-click in the middle area and select "New Image Set" as shown in Figure 7.17.

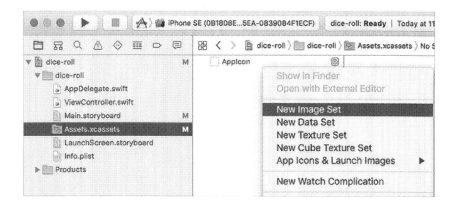

Figure 7.17. Creating a new image set

A new image set is now created. Click once on the "Image" text as shown in Figure 7.18 and it will be highlighted. Change its name to something meaningful such that you can easily access it from your code later (don't forget to hit return on your keyboard after renaming it). I named it as "dice-1".

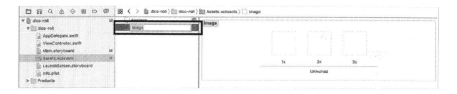

Figure 7.18. Renaming the image set

As you can see, there are three sizes for the new image set. If you insert only one image at 1x, then your app will use it everywhere you reference the image set name. Since there will be only one size for dice face images in our app, inserting an image only to 1x is OK.

In order to insert an image, drag it and drop to the 1x frame from the Finder of your Mac as shown in Figure 7.19.

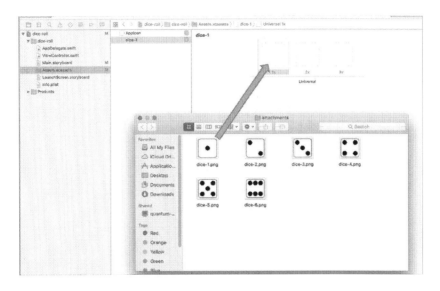

Figure 7.19. Inserting an image to the image dataset by drag and drop

Please repeat, "creating an image dataset, renaming it and inserting its image" procedure for each die face image. I have also added an image to display when the app first starts before any rolling operation. You can find it as "dice-general.png" on the book's website: www.yamaclis.com/ios11. After adding all these, you should have the assets file shown below:

Figure 7.20. Assets file after adding all die face images

After adding these images, you can set the default image of the image view object of the user interface by selecting the Main.storyboard file in Xcode and then clicking on the image view object as shown in Figure 7.21. Please select dice-general from the drop-down box as indicated by the arrow.

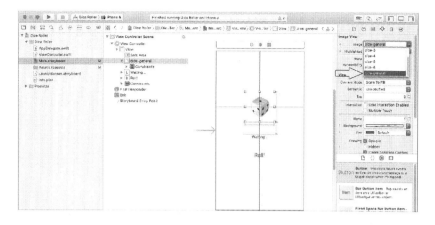

Figure 7.21. Setting the default image of the image view

You may have noted that there's an empty "AppIcon" image set in the assets file. If you insert an image there, it will be your app's icon that will be shown to the user on a real device.

## 7.3. Connecting UI Objects to the Code

We'll do the usual connecting procedure for the components of our user interface using the "Assistant editor" as explained in detail before. The connections of the image view and the label components will be of type **IBOutlet** while the connection type of the button will be **IBAction**. I named their connection names as "dieImage", "dieResult" and "rollDie", respectively. After the connections, the ViewController.swift file looks like below:

```
import UIKit

class ViewController: UIViewController {

    override func viewDidLoad() {
        super.viewDidLoad()
    }

    @IBOutlet weak var dieImage: UIImageView!
    @IBOutlet weak var dieResult: UILabel!
    @IBAction func rollDie(_ sender: Any) {
    }
    override func didReceiveMemoryWarning() {
        super.didReceiveMemoryWarning()
```

```
        }
}
```

Code 7.1 (cont'd from the previous page)

We'll write our main code inside the rollDie button's function since our app is not supposed to do anything until the user taps this button.

## 7.4. Randomness Function in Swift

Each time the user clicks on the "Roll!" button, the app has to generate a random number between 1 and 6. In Swift 4, we can generate random numbers with the built-in function **arc4random_uniform(x)** where x is an integer and the return value of this function is a random number between 0 and x-1. Therefore, in order to generate a random number between 1 and 6, we can employ this function as **arc4random_uniform(6) + 1**. Adding this code line to the ViewController.swift file and also including the usual label text setting, we have the code below:

```
import UIKit

class ViewController: UIViewController {

    override func viewDidLoad() {
        super.viewDidLoad()
    }
    @IBOutlet weak var dieImage: UIImageView!
    @IBOutlet weak var dieResult: UILabel!
    @IBAction func rollDie(_ sender: Any) {
        let randomNumber = arc4random_uniform(6) + 1
        self.dieResult.text = String(randomNumber)
    }
    override func didReceiveMemoryWarning() {
        super.didReceiveMemoryWarning()
    }
}
```

Code 7.2

## 7.5. Updating Images in the Code

Note that, the keyword **self** is used to access the **dieResult** label in Code 7.2 since we're accessing the label located in the storyboard related to this ViewController class. Now, we need to change the die image according to the generated random number. We can use if-else or switch-case statements. Since here are 6 possibilities, it is better to utilize a switch-case structure. In each of the cases, we can set the image with the code `self.dieImage.image = UIImage(named: "imageName")` where imageName is the image set's name we created in the assets file before. Incorporating the switch-case statements, the final code of our app can be given as below:

```
import UIKit
class ViewController: UIViewController {

    override func viewDidLoad() {
        super.viewDidLoad()
    }

@IBOutlet weak var dieImage: UIImageView!
@IBOutlet weak var dieResult: UILabel!
@IBAction func rollDie(_ sender: Any) {
let randomNumber = arc4random_uniform(6) + 1
self.dieResult.text = String(randomNumber)
switch randomNumber {
case 1:
 self.dieImage.image = UIImage(named: "dice-1")"
case 2:
 self.dieImage.image = UIImage(named: "dice-2")"
case 3:
 self.dieImage.image = UIImage(named: "dice-3")"
case 4:
 self.dieImage.image = UIImage(named: "dice-4")"
case 5:
 self.dieImage.image = UIImage(named: "dice-5")"
case 6:
 self.dieImage.image = UIImage(named: "dice-6")"
default:
 return
        }
    }

    override func didReceiveMemoryWarning() {
        super.didReceiveMemoryWarning()
    }
}
```

Code 7.3

## 7.6. Building and Running the App

Let's run our die roller app by hitting the "Run" button in Xcode. The user interface shown in Figure 7.22 appears. Each time we click the "Roll!" button, the app should show a different number with the corresponding die face image as in Figure 7.23.

It is worth noting that random numbers are not only used for fun apps but also in everyday cryptographic processes like online credit card transactions, etc. Hence there are much more sophisticated random number generation functions in Swift, also with the incorporation of external libraries. However for simple randomness like in our die rolling game, `arc4random_uniform` function seems adequate. You can check its randomness by consecutively clicking on the "Roll!" button and observing if you obtain the same number a lot or if the numbers show a pattern such that you can guess the next number. However, please keep in mind that accurate testing of randomness requires complex tools.

Figure 7.22. The user interface of the die rolling app when it's first run

Figure 7.23. Die rolling app showing 5 after one of the rollings

**Final note:** You can try to change the die rolling game to a food rolling game: change the die face images with pizza, burger, kebabs, etc. and roll to see what you'll order before you continue to the next chapter where we will develop our 4th app: the exercise calorie calculator.

# Chapter 8

# iOS APP # 4: EXERCISE CALORIE CALCULATOR

## 8.1. General Information

We have developed single view apps until now. However, tabbed apps also have a significant place in mobile development. In this chapter we will develop a tabbed app. This app will be a simple exercise calorie calculator that will be used to calculate the calories burned during a physical exercise. The app will have 3 tabs. In the first tab, the user will enter the constants: age, weight and gender information; in the second tab, exercise parameters will be entered: average heart rate and workout time. Finally, the burned calories will be calculated and displayed in the third tab. In this chapter, we'll learn how we can pass small data between tabs using global variables.

We'll use the following formulas for calculating the calories burned utilizing the input from the user (taken from: http://fitnowtraining.com/2012/01/formula-for-calories-burned/):

For women:

$$Burned\ calories = \left[\begin{array}{l}(Age\ x\ 0.074) - (Weight\ x\ 0.05741) \\ + (Heart\ rate\ x\ 0.04472) - 20.4022\end{array}\right] x\ Exer.\ time\ /\ 4.184$$

For men:

$$Burned\ calories = \left[\begin{array}{l}(Age\ x\ 0.2017) - (Weight\ x\ 0.09036) \\ + (Heart\ rate\ x\ 0.06309) - 55.0969\end{array}\right] x\ Exer.\ time\ /\ 4.184$$

Don't worry if equations make you dizzy, we won't go deep into how these equations are obtained or what we can do with them mathematically. We'll just use them in our app and I'll show you how we can easily implement these calculations in our Swift code.

## 8.2. Creating a Tabbed App

Start Xcode, select "Create a new Xcode project" and then choose the tabbed application as shown in Figure 8.1. Give a name to your project and save the project to the disk as usual.

Figure 8.1. Creating a tabbed application in Xcode

Xcode creates two view controllers and their corresponding Swift files by default when a tabbed app is created as shown in Figure 8.2.

## 8.3. Adding More Tabs

For this project, we need 3 tabs therefore we need to add one more view controller and its tab. To do this, select the Main.storyboard file. Then find the "View Controller" object from the object library and drag and drop it to somewhere empty in the storyboard viewer as shown in Figure 8.3.

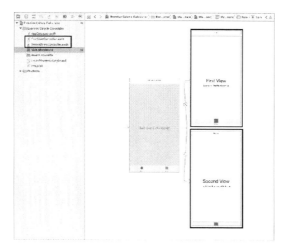

Figure 8.2. Tabbed app with 2 view controllers

After the drag and drop operation, the newly created empty view controller is shown in the storyboard as in Figure 8.4.

In order to be able to open the new view controller from the tab menu, we need to attach a tab bar item to it. Find the tab bar item from the object library and then drag-drop on the newly added empty view controller as in Figure 8.5.

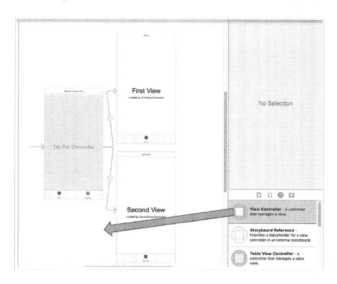

Figure 8.3. Drag and drop of a new view controller to the scene

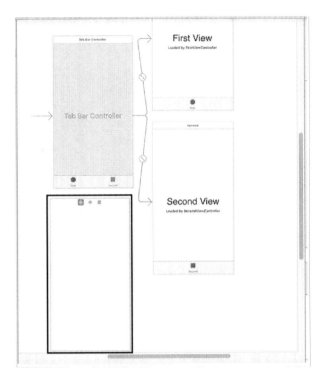

Figure 8.4. Newly added view controller in the storyboard

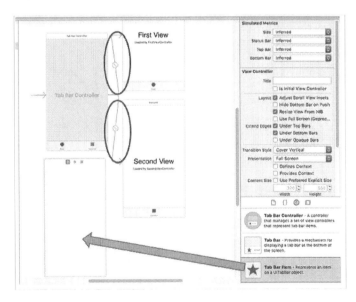

Figure 8.5. Adding a tab bar item to the new view controller

## 8.4. Connecting the New Tab to the Navigator

After adding the tab bar item, our view controller is ready to be a component of the tabbed app. However, the main tab bar controller shown by the grey screen in the storyboard doesn't know about the newly added view controller yet. We need to make a connection between the two. In fact as you may have noticed before, the view controllers are shown as connected to the tab view controller by big arrows as shown inside the ellipses in Figure 8.5. In order to connect the main tab bar controller to the new view controller, **hold down the control key** and then drag and drop a line from the greyed tab bar controller to the new empty view controller as in Figure 8.6. After dropping, Xcode will present you a menu as shown in Figure 8.7.

In the menu of Figure 8.7, select the "view controllers" option and then your new view controller will be connected to the tab bar controller as shown in Figure 8.8.

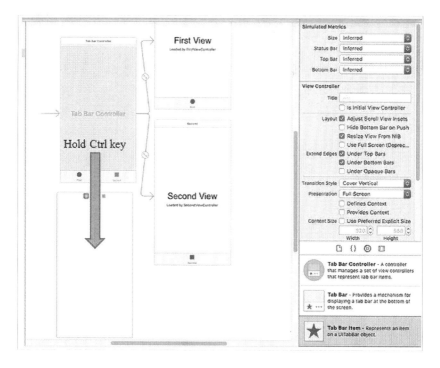

Figure 8.6. Connecting the tab bar controller and the new view controller

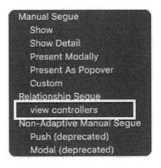

Figure 8.7. Connecting the new view controller using the "view controllers" option

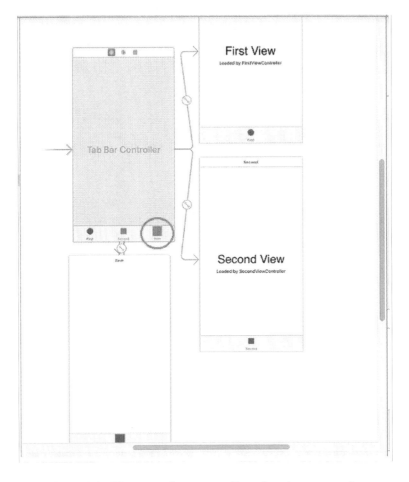

Figure 8.8. The new view controller after the connection

## 8.5. Connecting a New Class to the New Tab

Note that, the tab bar controller now shows the tab symbol of the new view controller as shown inside the circle in Figure 8.8. As you know there should be a Swift file corresponding to each view controller. However our new view controller doesn't have one yet. Let's create its class by right clicking on the file explorer as in Figure 8.9 and selecting "New File". In the next menu, **select "Swift File"** and give it a name accordingly like **ThirdViewController** as in Figures 8.10 and 8.11, respectively. After these steps, Xcode file explorer should look like Figure 8.12 where the new file is shown inside the rectangle.

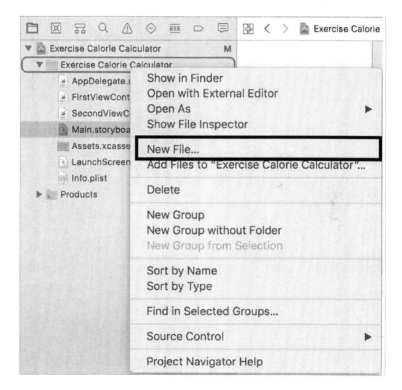

Figure 8.9. Adding a new file to the project

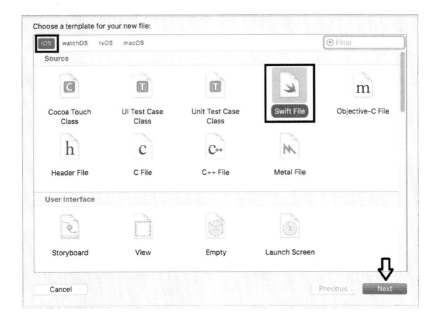

Figure 8.10. Selecting the file type

Figure 8.11. Naming the new file

Figure 8.12. Xcode file explorer after adding the new file

Now we have a new Swift file but it is empty as you can see by clicking on it. In order to connect the new view controller to this file, we need to create a new class in it. The easy way is copying the contents of one of the existing Swift files like FirstViewController.swift and then pasting it inside the new ThirdViewController.swift file. And then, let's change the name of the class to ThirdViewController. The contents of the ThirdViewController file will be as shown below:

```swift
import UIKit
class ThirdViewController: UIViewController {

    override func viewDidLoad() {
        super.viewDidLoad()
    }
    override func didReceiveMemoryWarning() {
        super.didReceiveMemoryWarning()
    }
}
```
Code 8.1

Now we need to attach the new view controller to the ThirdViewController.swift file we just created. For that, select Main.storyboard from the file explorer and the view controllers will be displayed. Select the new view controller **by clicking on the yellow circle called "Item"** as shown in Figure 8.13.

143

When the view controller is selected, find and select the "ThirdViewController" class from the "Identity inspector" tab at the right frame of Xcode as shown in Figure 8.14.

Let's run the project in the simulator to see what our app looks like at this stage. Hit the play button on Xcode and you should see the user interface shown in Figure 8.15.

Figure 8.13. Selecting the new view controller

Figure 8.14. Attaching the ThirdViewController class to the view controller

Figure 8.15. App's user interface at this stage

As you click on the tabs located at the bottom, you can navigate through the first, second and the newly added third view. However there's a problem: the last view's icon is missing, there's only one plain "Item" text for it. We can easily change the tab bar items to an image set already existing in Xcode or a custom image from an image set we can create. Let's select the tab item named "Item" on the newly added view controller and then set the icon for the third tab as the circle (first image existing in the assets file by default) and set its text as "Calculate calories" as we aimed in this project using the "Bar Item" menu from the right frame of Xcode as in Figure 8.16. I also changed the titles of the first and second tabs as "Enter personal info" and "Enter exercise info" with the same method. If we hit the play button in Xcode, our app's screens for different tabs should be as in Figure 8.17.

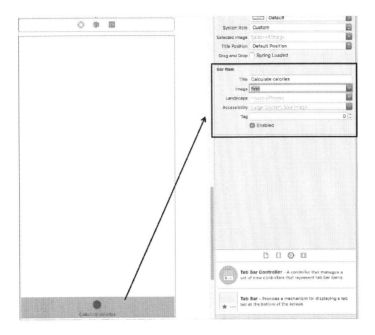

Figure 8.16. Setting the bar item's title and image

As you can see from Figure 8.17, the tabs of our app work perfectly. Now it's time for the usual interface design and coding. Currently our app's first two views have the default texts as set by Xcode and the third view has nothing in it, just a blank screen.

## 8.6. Adding a Segmented Control Object

We will enter text fields for the age and weight information. We can easily do this using our experience from previous chapters. Since I explained the text fields and labels in detail before, I won't do the same here in order not to make things boring for you. The only new component I added is a "Segmented Control" for selecting the gender info. A segmented control behaves as a two section button and it is easy to get its value in Swift. In order to add the segmented control, find it from the object library in Xcode as in Figure 8.18 and drag and drop on the screen. You can set its constraints as usual.

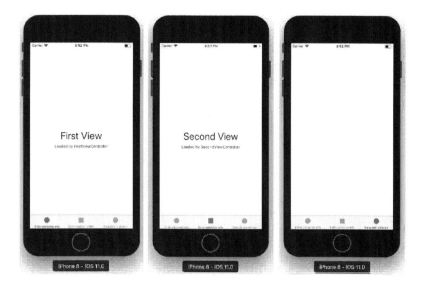

Figure 8.17. The app's different tabs

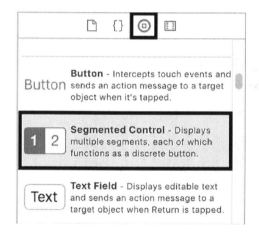

Figure 8.18. Adding a segmented control

Segmented control has two sections by default and they are named as "First" and "Second". Our gender info will also have two values: male and female hence we don't need to change the number of sections but the names. Select each section of the segmented control and then on the top right pane of Xcode, change the names to female and male, respectively as shown below:

147

Figure 8.19. Setting properties of the segmented control

Finally, add a button below the segmented control to save the personal information. After these changes, the screen for the first tab looks like Figure 8.20 (note that your screen layout may look significantly different as I didn't give the details about the positioning of the components).

Similarly, we need to add labels and text fields for the exercise time and the average heart rate in the second tab's view. I have designed a similar layout as shown in Figure 8.21 but you can design it as you like as long as it can take the needed information from the user.

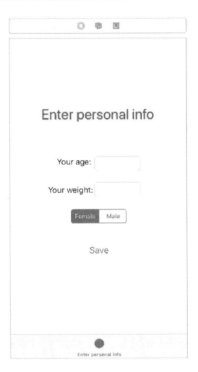

Figure 8.20. The storyboard of the first view

In the third tab we will just have a button to calculate the calories burned and a label to show the result. I designed it like in Figure 8.22. I know it looks plain, you can do some make up on it if you wish.

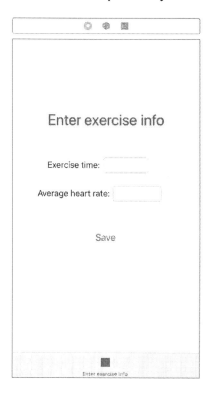

Figure 8.21. Layout of the second tab

## 8.7. Connecting UI Elements to the Code

We'll connect each view's components to their own classes located in FirstViewController.swift, SecondViewController.swift and ThirdViewController.swift for the first, second and the third tabs, respectively. We'll use **IBOutlet** for label, text fields and the segmented control and **IBAction** for the buttons and the segmented control of the first tab. Note that we need to add both an outlet and an action for the segmented control to take its value and get a trigger when the user taps on it. After the usual connections using the assistant editor of Xcode, the Swift files for all three tabs are as shown in Code 8.2, 8.3 and 8.4.

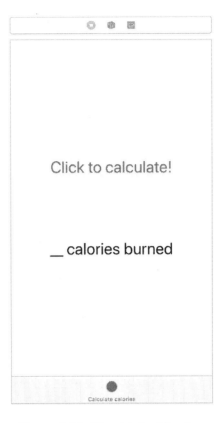

Figure 8.22. The third tab's view

```
import UIKit
class FirstViewController: UIViewController {
    override func viewDidLoad() {
        super.viewDidLoad()
    }
@IBOutlet weak var yourAge: UITextField!
@IBOutlet weak var yourWeight: UILabel!
@IBOutlet weak var genderButton: UISegmentedControl!
@IBAction func genderButton(_ sender: Any)
    }
@IBAction func savePersonalInfo(_ sender: Any) {
    }
override func didReceiveMemoryWarning() {
  super.didReceiveMemoryWarning()
    }
}
```
Code 8.2

```
import UIKit

class SecondViewController: UIViewController {

    override func viewDidLoad() {
        super.viewDidLoad()
    }

    @IBOutlet weak var exerciseTime: UITextField!
    @IBOutlet weak var avgHeartRate: UITextField!
    @IBAction func saveExerciseInfo(_ sender: Any) {
    }

    override func didReceiveMemoryWarning() {
        super.didReceiveMemoryWarning()
    }
}
```
Code 8.3

```
import UIKit
class ThirdViewController: UIViewController {
    override func viewDidLoad() {
        super.viewDidLoad()
    }
    @IBOutlet weak var calories: UILabel!

    @IBAction func calcCalories(_ sender: Any) {
    }
    override func didReceiveMemoryWarning() {
        super.didReceiveMemoryWarning()
    }
}
```
Code 8.4

## 8.8. Developing the Main Code

Now we are ready to write the actual code for calculating the calories burned. Since we need to pass data from the first and second tabs to the third tab for calculation (the calculation will take place when the user clicks the "Click to calculate calories burned" button in the third tab), we will define the variables that will contain the age, weight, gender, exercise time and heart rate information as global variables. Global variables are the variables that can be accessed from any code line in the project. Some programmers dislike using global variables since they may easily cause errors in big projects however there's no problem using global variables in our small project here. The ViewController.swift files after adding the global variables and the related calculation code are given in Code 8.5, Code 8.6 and Code 8.7, for the first, second and third views respectively. Note that we define global variables before the class definitions so that their scope won't be limited to that class.

```swift
import UIKit

var userAge: Double?
var userWeight: Double?
var userGender: String = "Female"
class FirstViewController: UIViewController {
    override func viewDidLoad() {
        super.viewDidLoad()
    }
@IBOutlet weak var yourAge: UITextField!
@IBOutlet weak var yourWeight: UITextField!
@IBOutlet weak var segmentedControl: UISegmentedControl!
@IBAction func genderButton(_ sender: Any) {
  switch genderButton.selectedSegmentIndex {
    case 0:
      userGender = "Female"
    case 1:
      userGender = "Male"
    default:
      return
        }
}
@IBAction func savePersonalInfo(_ sender: Any) {
        userWeight = Double(yourWeight.text!)
        userAge = Double(yourAge.text!)
    }
    override func didReceiveMemoryWarning() {
        super.didReceiveMemoryWarning()
    }
}
```
Code 8.5

Note that in Code 8.5, the "Save" button enables the variables "userWeight" and "userAge" to be set by the values entered in the respective text fields. On the other hand, the segmented control's action outlet sets the **userGender** variable to "Female" or "Male". Note that when one of the two sections (female and male) of the segmented control is clicked, the state of the segmented control is read by the method **selectSegmentIndex** which is applied on the outlet variable **segmentedControl**. The segment indices start with 0 and increase one by one. Since we have female at index 0 and male at index 1 in our example, case 0 will correspond to the female user while case 1 will indicate a male user. If the user is female, she will not click on the segmented control since it is set to female when the app starts. In order to cover this situation, **userGender** variable is set to "Female" at the start of the code by default.

```
import UIKit
var userExerciseTime: Double?
var userHeartRate: Double?
class SecondViewController: UIViewController {
    override func viewDidLoad() {
        super.viewDidLoad()
    }
    @IBOutlet weak var exerciseTime: UITextField!
    @IBOutlet weak var avgHeartRate: UITextField!
    @IBAction func saveExerciseInfo(_ sender: Any) {

        userExerciseTime = Double(exerciseTime.text!)
        userHeartRate = Double(avgHeartRate.text!)
    }
    override func didReceiveMemoryWarning() {
        super.didReceiveMemoryWarning()
        }
}
```
Code 8.6

The listing of the SecondViewController is given in Code 8.6. It just takes the values of the text fields "exerciseTime" and "avgHeartRate", converts them to Double type (since we'll do maths with them in the third tab) and stores them in the global variables named **userExerciseTime** and **userHeartRate** when the "Save" button is clicked.

```swift
import UIKit

var caloriesBurned: Double?
class ThirdViewController: UIViewController {

    override func viewDidLoad() {
        super.viewDidLoad()
    }

    @IBOutlet weak var calories: UILabel!

    @IBAction func calcCalories(_ sender: Any) {
switch userGender {
    case "Female":
      caloriesBurned = ((userAge!*0.074)-
      (userWeight!*0.05741)+(userHeartRate!*0.4472)-
      20.4022)*userExerciseTime!/4.184
    case "Male":
      caloriesBurned = ((userAge!*0.2017)-
      (userWeight!*0.09036)+(userHeartRate!*0.6309)-
      55.0969)*userExerciseTime!/4.184
    default:
       return
       }
       calories.text = String(Int(caloriesBurned!)) +
                                  "calories burned"
    }

    override func didReceiveMemoryWarning() {
        super.didReceiveMemoryWarning()
    }
}
```

Code 8.7

Code of the ThirdViewController is given in Code 8.7. When the "Click to calculate!" button is pressed, the burned calories are calculated in the switch-case statement depending on the gender (remember than burned calories are calculated using different formulas for male and female as given at the beginning of this chapter). The result is then displayed by the **caloriesBurned** label. It is also important to remember to unwrap optionals with (!) as you can see in this code listing.

## 8.9. Running the App

We have completed coding phase of our exercise calculator app. Let's run it on the simulator by pressing the "Run" button in Xcode. The screen shown in Figure 8.23 appears, which is the first tab for entering personal info. I entered the values shown in the figure and then clicked the save button. **Note that the formulas and our app use pounds as the weight unit.** Then, in the second tab, I entered the exercise info given in Figure 8.24 and again clicked the save button. Finally, in the third view of Figure 8.25, I clicked the button to calculate and the app gave the result of 154 calories. It's for 1 hour of exercise. **I verified the result by calculating the formula manually. The number is correct, just 154 calories!** Considering that an average sized burger has around 250 calories according to calorielab.com, I feel depressed now and will take a break to have a coffee before the next chapter where we will develop an app that uses GPS and map services.

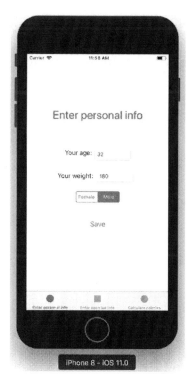

Figure 8.23. Entering personal info in the first view

Figure 8.24. Entering exercise info in the second view

Figure 8.25. Calories calculated by our app

**Note:** The app runs well on a real device; however as in the BMI Calculator app, the keyboard does not disappear after entering values. In order to make the keyboard disappear, we'll do the same trick we did in the BMI Calculator app (please see Note 4 in Chapter 6). The codes for the FirstViewController.swift and SecondviewController.swift files are shown in Code 8.8 and Code 8.9, respectively after adding the keyboard hiding method **textFieldShouldReturn**. When you update your code according to these, the keyboard should hide on a real device when the user clicks the "Return" button after entering her/his personal and exercise info. Remember that complete project files are available for download on the book's website: www.yamaclis.com/ios11.

```swift
import UIKit

var userAge: Double?
var userWeight: Double?
var userGender: String = "Female"

class FirstViewController: UIViewController, UITextFieldD
elegate {

    override func viewDidLoad() {
        super.viewDidLoad()
        self.yourAge.delegate = self
        self.yourWeight.delegate = self
    }
@IBOutlet weak var yourAge: UITextField!
@IBOutlet weak var yourWeight: UITextField!
@IBOutlet weak var segmentedControl: UISegmentedControl!
@IBAction func genderButton(_ sender: Any) {
        switch segmentedControl.selectedSegmentIndex {
        case 0:
            userGender = "Female"
        case 1:
            userGender = "Male"
        default:
            return
        }
    }
@IBAction func savePersonalInfo(_ sender: Any) {

    userWeight = Double(yourWeight.text!)
    userAge = Double(yourAge.text!)
    }
func textFieldShouldReturn(_ textField: UITextField) -
> Bool {
        self.yourWeight.resignFirstResponder()
```

```
        self.yourAge.resignFirstResponder()
        return true
    }

    override func didReceiveMemoryWarning() {
        super.didReceiveMemoryWarning()
    }
}
```

Code 8.8 (cont'd from the previous page)

```
import UIKit

var userExerciseTime: Double?
var userHeartRate: Double?

class SecondViewController: UIViewController, UITextField
Delegate {
override func viewDidLoad() {
        super.viewDidLoad()
        self.exerciseTime.delegate = self
        self.avgHeartRate.delegate = self
    }

@IBOutlet weak var exerciseTime: UITextField!
@IBOutlet weak var avgHeartRate: UITextField!
@IBAction func saveExerciseInfo(_ sender: Any) {

        userExerciseTime = Double(exerciseTime.text!)
        userHeartRate = Double(avgHeartRate.text!)
    }

func textFieldShouldReturn(_ textField: UITextField) -> Bool {
        self.exerciseTime.resignFirstResponder()
        self.avgHeartRate.resignFirstResponder()
        return true
    }

    override func didReceiveMemoryWarning() {
        super.didReceiveMemoryWarning()
    }
}
```

Code 8.9

Chapter 9

# iOS APP # 5: SHOW MY LOCATION: USING GPS AND MAPS

## 9.1. Creating the Project and Adding a Map Kit View

Geolocation and navigation apps are popular in all mobile platforms. Considering this, most mobile devices especially smartphones include components called GPS receivers. These receivers take microwave band radio signals from global positioning satellites that move in specified orbits around the earth. These GPS signals are extremely weak but thanks to the electronics tech, amplifier and processing circuits in smartphones can utilize these signals for location services.

Anyway, let's start developing our 5th app: Show My Location. In this chapter, you'll learn to use maps and geolocation data from GPS in your apps. It sounds easy but there are some confusing tricks to use the GPS receiver; don't worry I'll show all of them in a while.

In this app, we aim to show our location on the map while displaying the coordinate info just beneath the map in real time.

Let's start with creating a new project and saving it on the disk as usual. From the object library, place a label to show the title of your app and then find the object called "Map Kit View" and drag and drop it on the storyboard as in Figure 9.1.

A Map Kit View shows a map on the screen together with the annotations and other info we can place on the map. Most of the properties of the map are set programmatically.

We will show real time the latitude, longitude and altitude values besides the map in our app therefore I have added the required labels and text fields for these too as in Figure 9.2.

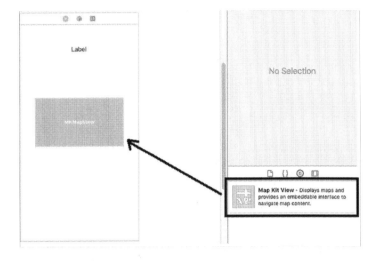

Figure 9.1. Adding a Map Kit View to the storyboard

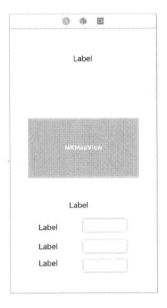

Figure 9.2. The layout template of the view

## 9.2. Adding the Constraints

We now have to edit the labels in the view and add constraints so that the components will not free float on the screen.

> **For the title label:** I have set the title's font size to 25 with the heavy option (remember that we do all these by selecting the component and then using the Attributes menu in the top right pane in Xcode). I centred the text inside the label and set the font colour as brown. Then I centred it horizontally with the "Align" menu as shown in Figure 9.3. Its distance to the top edge is set as 20 units while the width and height are given the values of 250 and 30 units, respectively from the "Pin" menu. These constraint settings are also given in Figure 9.4.

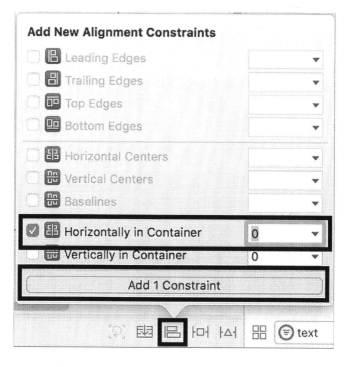

Figure 9.3. Centring the title label horizontally

> **The map:** Again, please align it horizontally from the "Align" menu as above and you can set the constraints as: distance to the nearest component above: 10 units, width and height: 300 units from the "Pin" menu. These settings are shown in Figure 9.5.

➤ **The labels and the text fields below the map:** I changed the text of the label just below the map as "Your coordinates" since we'll show the numerical coordinate info at this section. Its font size is set as 20 units and the text is centred. It is horizontally aligned and then the following constraints are added: distance to the component above: 25 units, width: 200 units, height: 25 units. These are shown in Figure 9.6.

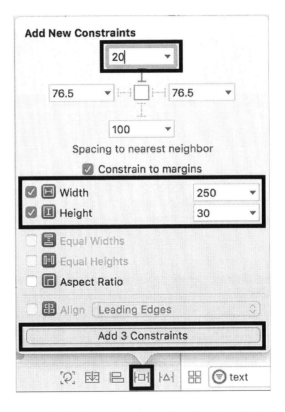

Figure 9.4. Setting the constraints for the title label

Three labels and associated three text fields are about the user's latitude, longitude and altitude. Hence the labels' texts are changed as "Latitude", "Longitude" and "Altitude" from top to down.

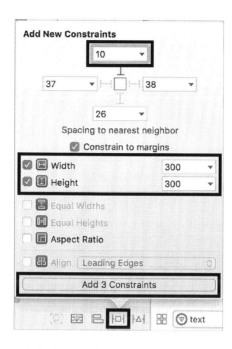

Figure 9.5. Constraints for the map component

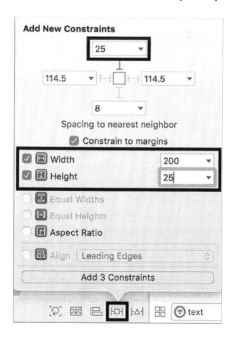

Figure 9.6. Constraints for the label just below the map

➢ **Constraints for the "Latitude" label** are set as follows: Distances to the nearest top and left components: 20 and 100 units; width and height are 77 and 21 units, respectively. These are shown in Figure 9.7.

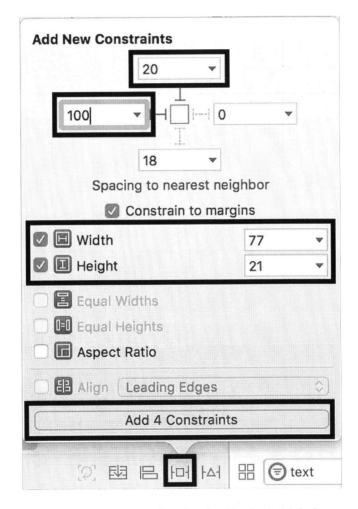

Figure 9.7. Constraints for the "Latitude" label

➢ **Text field next to the latitude label:** The distance to the nearest component to the left (the "Latitude" label) is 10 and width and height are 120 and 30 units, respectively, as in Figure 9.8. In order to align the "Latitude" label and the text field next to it vertically, please hold down the Command key on your keyboard, select the

"Latitude" label and its text field. Then from the "Pin" menu, select Align → Vertical centres and click "Add Constraint" button. If you update frames now, you should see that the label and its text field will be aligned vertically (on the same horizontal line).

➤ **The longitude label:** This is the label at the second row at the bottom section. Its constraints are set as follows: distances to the top and left components as 20 and 100 units; width and height as 87 and 21 units, respectively. These settings are shown in Figure 9.10.

➤ **Longitude text field:** The 3 constraints for the longitude text field are defined as: distance to the left item: 0, width: 120 and height 30 units as in Figure 9.11. The vertical axes of the longitude label and longitude text field are aligned as we did for the latitude components before. Hence, both label and the text field for the longitude are completely positioned.

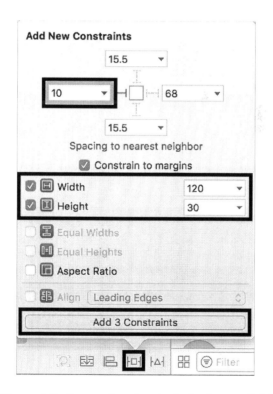

Figure 9.8. Constraints for the latitude text field

➢ **Altitude label and the text field:** The settings for these components are the same as the longitude label and component, respectively except that the distance of the altitude text field to the label at its left is 18 units instead of 10 units. After completing all the constraints, the main view of your app should look like Figure 9.12.

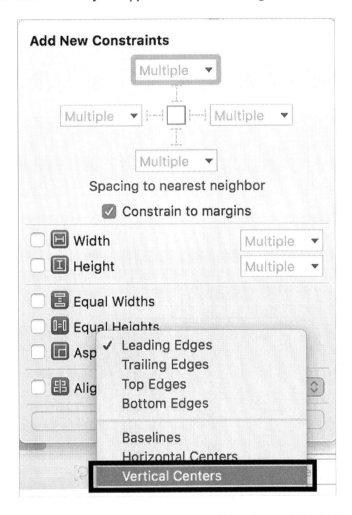

Figure 9.9. Aligning the vertical centres of the "Latitude" label and its text view from the "Pin" menu

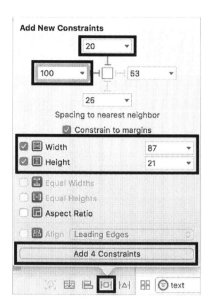

Figure 9.10. Settings for the "Longitude" label

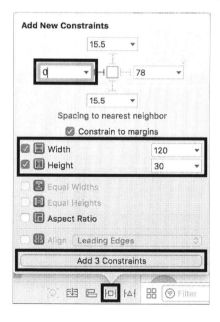

Figure 9.11. Settings for the longitude text field

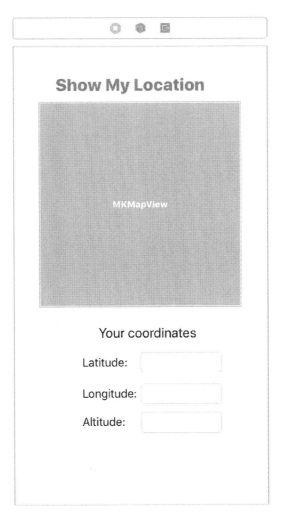

Figure 9.12. Finalized storyboard of our app

## 9.3. Adding Required Permissions

We'll set the properties of the map kit now. Let's start with setting the permissions for GPS and location services so that our app can use the GPS receiver on a real device. For this, single-click the Info.plist file on Xcode and then in the "Required Device Capabilities" tab, click the plus button as shown in Figure 9.13.

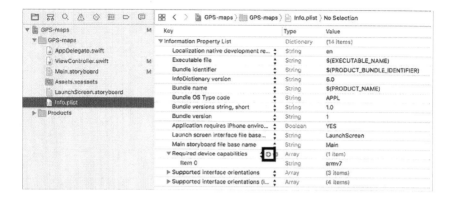

Figure 9.13. Adding the required device capabilities

Please add the text "gps" and then hit enter in the field which opens after the plus button is clicked. Do the same operation and write "location-services" this time. After these 2 steps, your Info.plist file should look like below:

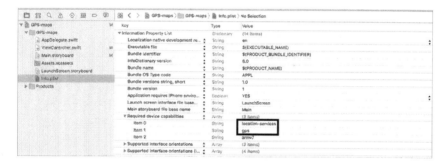

Figure 9.14. Info.plist file after adding the required device capabilities

In the next step, click on the plus button next to the "Information Property List" in Info.plist file and then select "Privacy-Location When In Use Usage Description" as in Figure 9.15.

Figure 9.15. Adding the location services popup info

After adding this property, we can set a text in the "Value" section that will be shown to the user in the GPS usage permission dialog box. I added the text "This app needs GPS signals to run." as shown below:

Figure 9.16. Finalized Info.plist file

## 9.4. Adding the Map Kit Library

We have added the required permissions. We can now add the library of map-related functions that already exists in Xcode. For this, select the main project tab in the left pane and then click on the "Build Phases" tab in the main pane; select the "Link Binary with Libraries" section and then click on the plus button. The order of this operation is shown in Figure 9.17.

Figure 9.17. Steps to add a library to the project

When you click on the plus button, a menu appears where you can select built-in libraries. In the search box type "map", click on the MapKit.framework and then click on the "Add" button to add the map library to the project as shown in Figure 9.18.

## 9.5. Connecting the Map Kit View to the Code

It's now time to connect the storyboard components to the ViewController.swift file. We have done this several times so I don't expect a problem. We need to connect the map and the 3 text field to the code since the remaining storyboard components are the labels that won't change when the app runs. Please connect the 3 text fields and the map as outlets. You can connect the map to the code as usual. The ViewController.swift file after connecting these objects is as shown as below:

```swift
import UIKit
class ViewController: UIViewController {
    override func viewDidLoad() {
        super.viewDidLoad()
    }
    @IBOutlet weak var myMap: MKMapView!
    @IBOutlet weak var myLatitude: UITextField!
    @IBOutlet weak var myLongitude: UITextField!
    @IBOutlet weak var myAltitude: UITextField!
    override func didReceiveMemoryWarning() {
        super.didReceiveMemoryWarning()
}}
```
Code 9.1

Figure 9.18. Adding the map library to the project

Xcode will show an error at the map outlet line. It is because we have included the MapKit Framework in the project however we didn't import it in our code yet. Hence, before the class definition (just after the **import UIKit** line), add the following line and the error will be gone:

```
import MapKit
```
Code 9.2

## 9.6. Main Code

We made the component connections and added the map library in the code. We can now write our main code for the operation of the GPS and location services to pinpoint our position on the map, give our coordinates in degrees and the altitude in metres.

First of all, in order to use the map related functions we need to extend our ViewController class with a class called **CLLocationManagerDelegate** by adding it in the class definition as in Code 9.3.

```
class ViewController: UIViewController, CLLocationManagerDelegate
```
Code 9.3

Note that we added the newly added class name after a comma. By inheriting from this class, we can use everything included in **CLLocationManagerDelegate** in our code.

We need three Double type variables that will hold the latitude, longitude and altitude information. We can define optionals for this just after the class definition as in Code 9.4.

```
var latitude: Double?
var longitude: Double?
var altitude: Double?
```
Code 9.4

Then we define an instance of **CLLocationManager** that will hold all information regarding the location as follows:

```
let locationManager = CLLocationManager()
```
Code 9.5

The **locationManager** object should start tracking the location as soon as the app loads. Therefore we need to place the initial operations regarding the start of the location tracking in the **viewDidLoad()** function. In this way the app will ask for location tracking and start tracking when the app first fires before any user intervention. We do this as in Code 9.6.

```
override func viewDidLoad() {
        super.viewDidLoad()
        locationManager.delegate = self
        locationManager.requestWhenInUseAuthorization()
        locationManager.startUpdatingLocation()
}
```
Code 9.6

This code will ask for user permission to track location and then start updating the location info. Next, we will use one of the built-in instance methods for checking if the GPS authorization status is changed. This function is shown in Code 9.7. If the GPS is enabled, it will print "GPS allowed." text in the Xcode terminal and will start showing your location on the map; otherwise it will print "GPS not allowed." in the Xcode terminal and will exit when you run the app in the simulator.

```
func locationManager(_ manager: CLLocationManager,
didChangeAuthorization status: CLAuthorizationStatus)
{
        if status == .authorizedWhenInUse {
            print("GPS allowed.")
            myMap.showsUserLocation = true
        }
        else {
            print("GPS not allowed.")
            return
        }}
```
Code 9.7

Finally, we will use another instance method to update the position info (latitude, longitude and altitude) written in the respective text fields. This method is shown in Code 9.8.

```
func locationManager(_ manager: CLLocationManager,
didUpdateLocations locations: [CLLocation]) {

let myCoordinate=locationManager.location?.coordinate
        altitude = locationManager.location?.altitude
        latitude = myCoordinate?.latitude
        longitude = myCoordinate?.longitude
        myLatitude.text = String(latitude!)
        myLongitude.text = String(longitude!)
        myAltitude.text = String(altitude!)
    }
```
Code 9.8.

In the fourth line of this code, the combined latitude and longitude info is taken from the location object and stored in **myCoordinate** constant. In the fifth line, altitude of the user is extracted and saved in the **altitude** variable. In the next two lines, combined latitude and longitude info are extracted from the **myCoordinate** constant. The rest is obvious, the text fields in the user interface are populated by the coordinate info.

The complete ViewController.swift is shown in Code 9.9.

```swift
import UIKit
import MapKit
class ViewController: UIViewController, CLLocationManage
rDelegate {
    var latitude: Double?
    var longitude: Double?
    var altitude: Double?
    let locationManager = CLLocationManager()
    @IBOutlet weak var myMap: MKMapView!
    @IBOutlet weak var myLatitude: UITextField!
    @IBOutlet weak var myLongitude: UITextField!
    @IBOutlet weak var myAltitude: UITextField!

    override func viewDidLoad() {
        super.viewDidLoad()
        locationManager.delegate = self
        locationManager.requestWhenInUseAuthorization()
        locationManager.startUpdatingLocation()
    }
    func locationManager(_ manager: CLLocationManager,
didChangeAuthorization status: CLAuthorizationStatus) {

        if status == .authorizedWhenInUse {
print("GPS allowed.")
            myMap.showsUserLocation = true
        }
        else {
            print("GPS not allowed.")
            return
        }
    }
    func locationManager(_ manager: CLLocationManager,
didUpdateLocations locations: [CLLocation]) {
        let myCoordinate = locationManager.location?.coordinate
        altitude = locationManager.location?.altitude
        latitude = myCoordinate?.latitude
        longitude = myCoordinate?.longitude

        myLatitude.text = String(latitude!)
        myLongitude.text = String(longitude!)
        myAltitude.text = String(altitude!)
    }
    override func didReceiveMemoryWarning() {
```

```
        super.didReceiveMemoryWarning()
        // Dispose of any resources that can be
recreated.
    }
}
```

Code 9.9 (cont'd from the previous page)

## 9.7. Running the App

When we hit the "Run" button in Xcode and run the app in the simulator, we are presented by the screen shown in Figure 9.19. The simulator cannot of course take GPS signals but a simulated location is shown on the map. The default location is the location of Apple HQ which is seen in Figure 9.19. If you install this app on a real iOS device, it will obviously show your actual location, not a simulated one.

You can change the simulated location from the simulator's "Debug" menu as shown in Figure 9.20 and Fisure 9.21. I entered the coordinates of a location at (41.3809° N, 2.1228° E) and the simulator shows it on the map as in Figure 9.21. Can you guess what this famous location is?

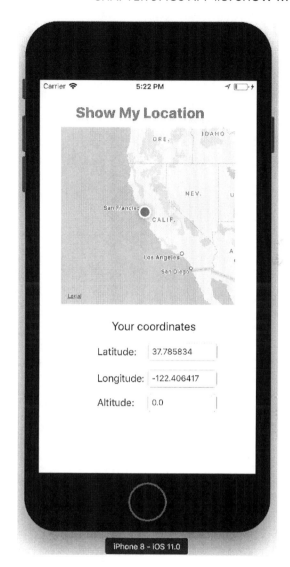

Figure 9.19. Developed "Show My Location" app in the simulator

## 9.8. Final Notes

**Final note 1.** I have installed the app on a real iPhone SE and it works as expected.

**Final note 2.** You cannot change the simulated altitude in the simulator.

**Final note 3.** If you're planning to go for a safari and use this app there wait until the next chapter where I'll show you sending text messages in Swift. We'll combine SMS sending and location services to develop an app that can be used for sending user's location to a pre-defined phone number easily in case of emergency.

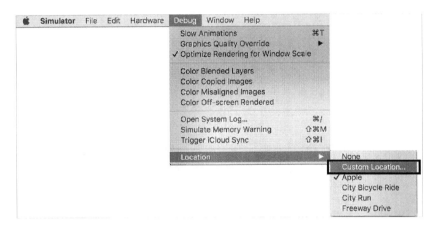

Figure 9.20. Changing the simulated coordinates in the simulator

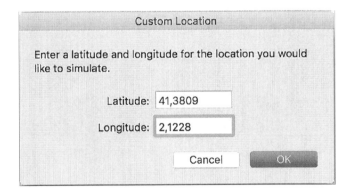

Figure 9.21. Entering new coordinates to the simulator

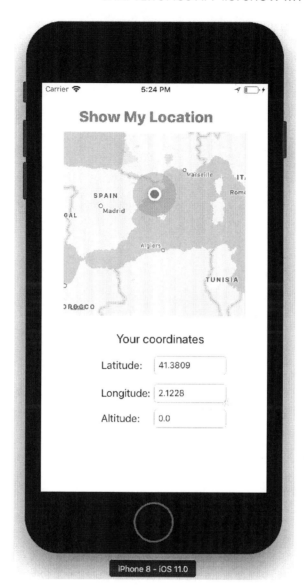

Figure 9.22. Developed app showing a famous point as a simulated location

# Chapter 10

# iOS APP # 6: S.O.S. MESSAGE SENDER

## 10.1. Copying a Project

Most of the iOS devices have the capability of GSM connection hence it is important to learn using SMS messaging in iOS. A class called **MFMessageComposeViewController** enables us to design apps that can open the native SMS messaging application of an iOS device with pre-populated recipient and message body fields and send an SMS with a single click. You'll see how this class is used in this chapter.

We'll develop an app which sends the current location using SMS to pre-defined recipients. This app can be useful in case of an emergency in deserts or if you're boozed in a disco when you cannot type text in the message field and need to send your location to a mate to take you home.

We'll extend the app that we developed in the previous chapter, find my location, since we'll send the location of the user and find my location app readily gives us the coordinates of the user. We'll wrap these coordinates and use the **MFMessageComposeViewController** class to send it via SMS. We need to duplicate the "Find My Location" app. For this, find the folder of the project on your Mac and duplicate this folder by right-clicking on it and selecting "Duplicate". A new folder with the name "(project name) copy" will be created. Now, select File → Open in Xcode's top bar and select the  new folder you created. We need to rename the project and attach a new bundle identifier to build and run it. For this, select the project from the left pane of Xcode as in Figure 10.1 and rename it something you want from the right pane of Xcode as shown in Figure 10.2.

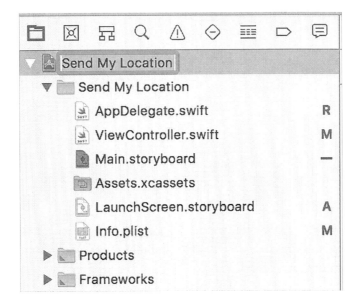

Figure 10.1. Selecting the project in Xcode

Figure 10.2. Renaming the project in Xcode

After you rename the project, Xcode will ask if you also want to rename files in your project. Select "Rename" in that dialog and then you'll have a copy of your previous project with a new name. After then, in the middle pane, change the bundle identifier to something you prefer as in Figure 10.3.

## 10.2. Adding New Objects

Let's open the Main.storyboard file and rename the app title and remove the big map object so that we can place a big "S.O.S." button. I renamed the app title as "Send My Location" and laid down a big button as in Figure 10.4. I also deleted the coordinate information labels and text fields since in case of emergency the user won't need to check those numbers. The final layout of the user interface is as in Figure 10.4.

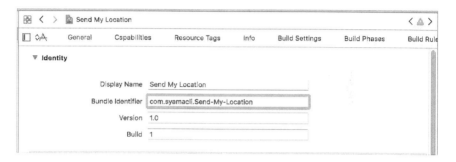

Figure 10.3. Changing bundle identifier

Now, before making any connection, delete all lines related to the previously deleted text fields. After cleaning up, the ViewController.swift file looks like in Code 10.1.

Code 10.1 is the plain version of the code of the app developed in the previous chapter. In its current phase, the **latitude** and **longitude** variables store the coordinate information. Now, we need to connect the big button to the code. Open up the "Assistant Editor" and connect this button as an IBAction. I named the connection as **sendButton**.

Figure 10.4. User interface of the app

```
import UIKit
import MapKit

class ViewController: UIViewController,
CLLocationManagerDelegate {

    var latitude: Double?
    var longitude: Double?
    let locationManager = CLLocationManager()
    override func viewDidLoad() {
    super.viewDidLoad()
        locationManager.delegate = self
        locationManager.requestWhenInUseAuthorization()
        locationManager.startUpdatingLocation()
    }

    func locationManager(_ manager: CLLocationManager,
```

```
didChangeAuthorization status: CLAuthorizationStatus) {

        if status == .authorizedWhenInUse {
            print("GPS allowed.")
        }
        else {
            print("GPS not allowed.")
            return
        }
    }
    func locationManager(_ manager: CLLocationManager,
didUpdateLocations locations: [CLLocation]) {
        let myCoordinate =
locationManager.location?.coordinate
        latitude = myCoordinate?.latitude
        longitude = myCoordinate?.longitude
    }

    override func didReceiveMemoryWarning() {
        super.didReceiveMemoryWarning()
    }
}
```

Code 10.1 (cont'd from the previous page)

## 10.3. Adding the SMS Library

We will now add the SMS library. For this, select the MessageUI binary in the Build Phases tab (explained in detail in the previous chapter) of the project properties as shown in Figure 10.5. The "Link binary with Libraries" section looks like in Figure 10.6 after adding this library.

Figure 10.5. Adding the MessagesUI framework

185

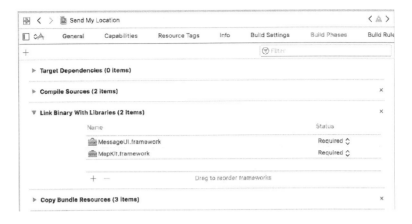

Figure 10.6. The "Build Phases" tab after adding the SMS library

## 10.4. Adding the Required Delegate Class

In order to use the newly added library, we will add the `import MessageUI` line at the beginning of our code and then inherit from the `MFMessageComposeViewControllerDelegate` class. After these insertions, the beginning of your Swift file should look like below:

```
import UIKit
import MapKit
import MessageUI

class ViewController: UIViewController,
CLLocationManagerDelegate,
MFMessageComposeViewControllerDelegate{
```
Code 10.2

Just after you add the class extensions, Xcode will give an error saying "The ViewController does not conform to protocol MFMessageComposeViewControllerDelegate". Don't worry about this. It means that we didn't include the required methods to conform to the `MFMessageComposeViewControllerDelegate` class. Now we'll add all the required methods.

## 10.5. Main Code

First of all, let's define a new instance of the messaging class as in Code 10.3 just after the previous variable definitions.

```
let messageCompose = MFMessageComposeViewController()
```
Code 10.3

Now, we'll define a new function as shown in Code 10.4. This function checks if the user's device can send SMS messages. It returns **true** if the user can send SMS and **false** otherwise.

```
func canSendText() -> Bool {
        return
MFMessageComposeViewController.canSendText()
}
```
Code 10.4

We'll use Code 10.5 as the button's function, which will actually prepare for SMS sending.

```
@IBAction func sendButton(_ sender: Any) {

messageCompose.messageComposeDelegate = self
messageCompose.recipients = ["0123456789"]
let SMSText = "Please take me from this location:
Latitude:" + String(latitude!) + " Longitude: " +
String(longitude!)
        messageCompose.body =  SMSText
        present(messageCompose, animated: true,
completion: nil)
    }
```
Code 10.5

The recipients and the message text are defined in this function. You should change the recipient number to the number you want to send your coordinates. You can define more than one number to send the coordinates as an array. The message body will read: ""Please take me from this location: Latitude:" + String(latitude!) + " Longitude: " + String(longitude!)" where your latitude and longitude info will be populated with your actual location.

This code opens the message composing interface for the user to send the coordinates. Note that iOS does not let you to send SMS in the background, it opens up the standard messaging interface and wants the user to be in control by finally clicking the "Send" button there.

187

In the end, we'll write the method which will tell the message delegate that the message composing is finished (after the user sends the message) as follows:

```
func messageComposeViewController(_ controller:
MFMessageComposeViewController, didFinishWith result:
MessageComposeResult) {
        controller.dismiss(animated: true, completion:
nil)
    }
```
Code 10.6

The complete ViewController.swift file is shown below:

```
import UIKit
import MapKit
import MessageUI
class ViewController: UIViewController,
CLLocationManagerDelegate,
MFMessageComposeViewControllerDelegate{

    var latitude: Double?
    var longitude: Double?
    let locationManager = CLLocationManager()
    let messageCompose =
MFMessageComposeViewController()
    override func viewDidLoad() {
        super.viewDidLoad()
locationManager.delegate = self
        locationManager.requestWhenInUseAuthorization()
        locationManager.startUpdatingLocation()
    }

    func locationManager(_ manager: CLLocationManager,
didChangeAuthorization status: CLAuthorizationStatus) {

        if status == .authorizedWhenInUse {
            print("GPS allowed.")
        }
        else {
            print("GPS not allowed.")
            return
        }
    }
```

CHAPTER 10. IOS APP #6: S.O.S. MESSAGE SENDER

```
    func locationManager(_ manager: CLLocationManager,
didUpdateLocations locations: [CLLocation]) {
        let myCoordinate =
locationManager.location?.coordinate
        latitude = myCoordinate?.latitude
        longitude = myCoordinate?.longitude

    }

    func canSendText() -> Bool {
        return
MFMessageComposeViewController.canSendText()
    }
    @IBAction func sendButton(_ sender: Any) {

        messageCompose.messageComposeDelegate = self
        messageCompose.recipients = ["xxxxxxxxxxx"]
//Enter a valid phone number here
let SMSText = "Please take me from this location:
Latitude:" + String(latitude!) + " Longitude: " +
String(longitude!)
        messageCompose.body =  SMSText
        present(messageCompose, animated: true,
completion: nil)

    }

    func messageComposeViewController(_ controller:
MFMessageComposeViewController, didFinishWith result:
MessageComposeResult) {
        controller.dismiss(animated: true, completion:
nil)
    }

    override func didReceiveMemoryWarning() {
        super.didReceiveMemoryWarning()
        // Dispose of any resources that can be
recreated.
    }
}
```

Code 10.7 (cont'd from the previous pages)

## 10.6. Running the App

If you try to run the app in a simulator, it will give a warning saying that it cannot send text messages, which is obvious. You need to try this app in a real device with SMS sending capability. I tried on iPhone SE and iPhone 7, they both worked fine. When I tap the S.O.S. button, a new SMS composing window opens with the recipient box pre-populated and the message body is a text of my latitude and longitude info. It sends the location info as expected.

Now, let's take a break and get a coffee. In the next chapter, we'll develop another exciting app: a 2D game ☺.

# Chapter 11

# iOS APP # 7: OUR iOS GAME: BOUNCE THE BALL

## 11.1. Creating the Game Project and Basic Settings

As we know, games are among the most popular apps. Game developers can earn good money once the gamers get addicted to their games. However, developing a game is not a simple task since a good game should have an exciting story, good graphics, realistic physics rules and efficient code to glue all these together. Fortunately, the game development framework named SpriteKit™ makes our lives easier. SpriteKit has functions and methods for both generating nice graphics and the accurate simulation of game objects according to physics rules. SpriteKit is built-in Xcode 9 hence we can easily start developing iOS games.

In this last chapter, we'll put all our knowledge and SpriteKit in action to develop a simple 2D game: Bounce the Ball. The idea is simple: a ball will move on the scene and the gamer will try to prevent the ball from touching the bottom edge of the screen by bouncing the ball with a paddle that he/she controls with screen touches.

First of all, to create a new Xcode *game project*, select "Game" as the application type as shown in Figure 11.1 and then click "Next". Name your project and then select "SpriteKit" as the game technology in the next window as in Figure 11.2. Save the project on your computer and then you'll see the project file explorer as shown in Figure 11.3 in the left pane of Xcode.

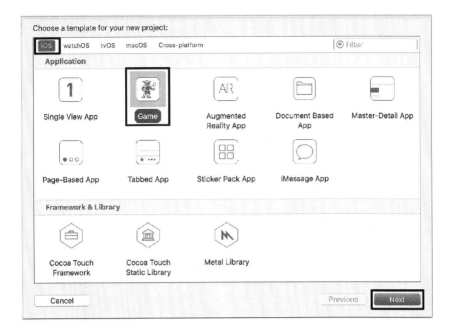

Figure 11.1. Creating a game project

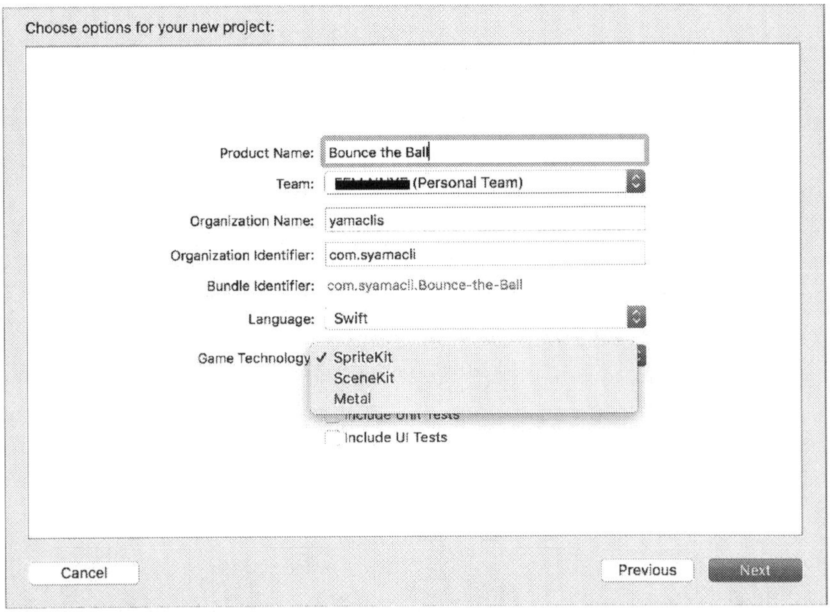

Choose options for your new project:

Product Name: Bounce the Ball

Team: ▓▓▓▓▓▓ (Personal Team)

Organization Name: yamacli

Organization Identifier: com.syamacli

Bundle Identifier: com.syamacli.Bounce-the-Ball

Language: Swift

Game Technology: ✓ SpriteKit
SceneKit
Metal

Include Unit Tests
Include UI Tests

Cancel    Previous Next

Figure 11.2. Selecting the game technology

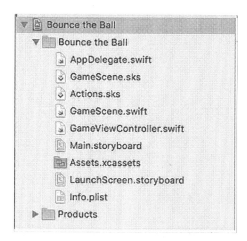

Figure 11.3. Default files of a game project

Comparing these files to the files of the general Xcode project shows that there is a new file type: .sks file. These are SpriteKit Scene files where you can use to visually design the scenes of your game. The code related to game functionality resides in Gamescene.swift and GameViewController.swift files. When you single-click on GameScene.sks file, you'll be presented by the default scene shown in Figure 11.4. In this scene, there's only a default label object that is similar to the label in UIView class. Labels display text in SpriteKit as in other projects. We won't need a label for now in our Bounce the Ball game therefore right-click the label from the scene browser and Delete as shown in Figure 11.5.

For a ball bouncing game, it is obviously better to set the screen in landscape mode. Select the project from the left pane of Xcode and then find the "Deployment Info" section as in Figure 11.6. Here, set the screen orientation as "Landscape Right" and then uncheck the "Portrait" mode.

Open the GameScene.sks again to set the screen size from the Scene Attributes found at the right top pane of Xcode as in Figure 11.7. I selected iPhone SE and Landscape mode but you can select any device you wish.

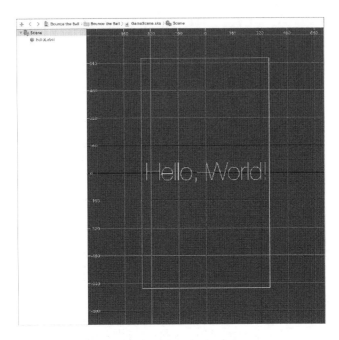

Figure 11.4. Default scene

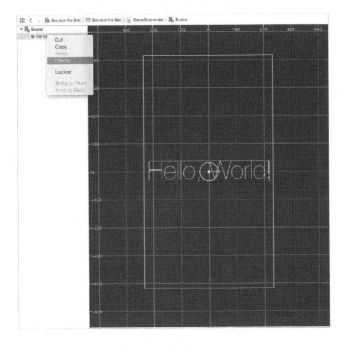

Figure 11.5. Deleting the default Label

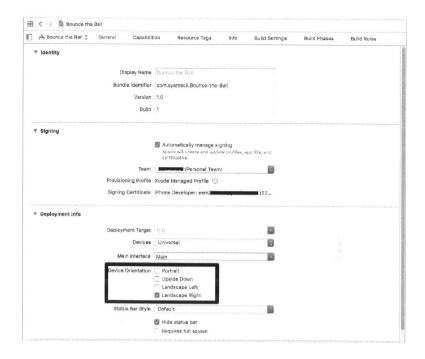

Figure 11.6. Setting the screen orientation in project settings

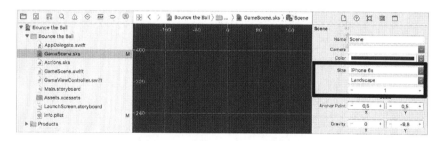

Figure 11.7. Setting screen size and the orientation in the scene attributes pane

In order to place objects in our game scene, we need to import them as images or data sets in the Assets.xcassets file as we did in previous projects. Open this file by single-clicking on it and then delete the default Spaceship image set. There will be only three objects (hence their images) in our simple game: the background, the ball and the paddle that will bounce the ball. In order to make things funny, I selected a red football shoe as the paddle. The ball is a football ball and the background

195

is a nice spring panorama. You can download these images from the book's website: www.yamaclis.com/ios11. Please create new image sets named background, ball and the shoe and place corresponding images to these data sets by drag and drop method. After these operations, your Assets.xcassets file should look like below (creating image sets was explained in detail in previous chapters, e.g. Chapter 7):

Figure 11.8. Assets.xcassets file after creating image sets

Now, open the GameScene.sks again to set the background image. For this, add a "Color Sprite" to the screen (by drag and drop) from the Objects library as shown in Figure 11.9.

We'll set this Sprite as the background image. Select this Sprite and then you can set its properties from the Sprite menu at the right top pane of Xcode. Select its Texture as "background" (name of the image set) and set Sprite's name to "background" (any name can be given) as shown in Figure 11.10.

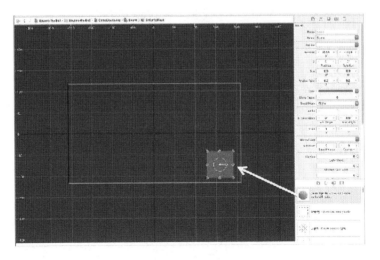

Figure 11.9. Adding a colour Sprite to the scene

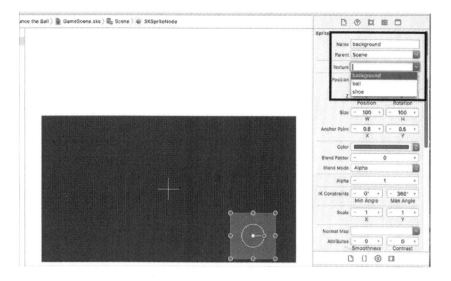

Figure 11.10. Setting the newly added Sprite's properties

The background image is very big compared to our screen size therefore we need to squeeze it to fit. Again in the Sprite menu, set its size to Width: 667 and Height: 375 for iPhone 8 as shown below (if you're designing your game for another device, read the next paragraph please):

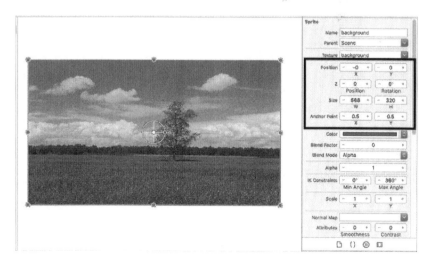

Figure 11.11. Setting the size of the background Sprite

If you're designing your game for a device other than iPhone 6S, then you you'll need to enter *its mapped screen size* which is shown in Table 11.1 (sources: http://www.kylejlarson.com/blog/iphone-6-screen-size-web-design-tips/ and http://iosres.com/). Since the screen orientation is set as landscape, the width value will be the bigger number and the height value will be the smaller number like W=568 and H=320 for iPhone SE.

| | iPhone 5/5S/SE | iPhone 6/6S/7/8 | iPhone 6/6S/7/8 Plus | iPhone X |
|---|---|---|---|---|
| **Physical Size** | 4 in | 4.7 in | 5.5 in | 5.8 in |
| *Mapped size* | *320 x 568 points* | *375 x 667 points* | *414 x 736 points* | *375 x 812 points* |
| **Rendered Pixels** | 640x1136 | 750x1334 | 1242x2208 | 1125x2436 |

Table 11.1. Screen sizes of various iOS devices

Note that, the position of the background Sprite has to be (0,0) to fill the screen properly. Now, run the game in the simulator to check if everything is going well as shown below:

Figure 11.12. The scene in the simulator

## 11.2. Adding the Ball

Let's add the ball to the scene to make our game more exciting ☺. Add a new Sprite from the Object Explorer and select its texture as "ball" (name of the image set), also set the Sprite's name as "ball" as in Figure 11.13. You can drag the ball anywhere you want in the scene (this will be the (x,y) position of the ball and the game will start with the ball in this position).

Since the ball is very big for the screen size, I adjusted the size of the ball as W=30 and H=30 (in fact this is the size of the Sprite that contains the ball).

**Important:** The z position of Sprites should be set properly otherwise they may randomly disappear during gameplay. The default z position of the background Sprite was 0 so it is OK to set the z position of the ball as 1. These settings are shown below:

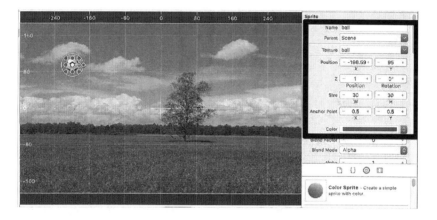

Figure 11.13. Adding the ball and setting its basic properties

## 11.3. Sprite Physics – Moving the Ball

The interactions of Sprites are defined by the physics laws that we set for the game scene and the Sprites themselves. For example, we can set a scene with no gravity or half gravity. Of course, Sprite physics is not only about gravity, it defines the effects of Sprites on each other and many other things. Setting the physics of the scene is in fact a vital part of game development.

Let's see how we define physics of the ball so that when we first run the app, the ball will not stay at its initial place but start moving and bouncing.

Select the ball and then find the section called "Physics Definition" in Xcode's right pane as shown below:

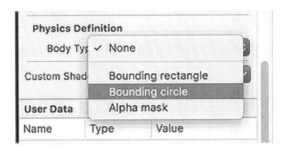

Figure 11.14. Physics definition pane

Select body type as "Bounding circle" as shown in the above figure and then a menu to set "physics properties" related to the ball Sprite will appear as in Figure 11.15 with default values.

The settings shown here can be summarized as follows:

➤ **Dynamic checkbox:** Determines if the Sprite will be affected by collisions etc.
➤ **Allows Rotation:** Determines if the Sprite may rotate dependent on the collision direction.
➤ **Pinned:** Sets if the Sprite will move or not in the scene.
➤ **Affected by Gravity:** Sets if the default gravity of the scene will affect this Sprite or not.
➤ **Friction:** Determines the frictional force the Sprite applies to other bodies – roughness of the Sprite.
➤ **Restitution:** This section sets the ratio of (the energy the Sprite gains after a collision) to (its initial energy). In other words, if this is 1, the collision is perfectly elastic otherwise the Sprite will lose energy when it hits somewhere/something during the gameplay. Also defined as the Sprite's bounciness.

➢ **Linear and Angular Dampings:** The "frictional constants" affecting the Sprite's velocity as it moves, the linear and angular parts of this force are set here. If these are nonzero, the Sprite will lose energy as it moves in the scene.

➢ **Mass:** A Sprite's resistance to acceleration under an applied force like the mass in real life.

➢ **Initial velocity:** The velocity the Sprite will have at the beginning of the game. DX and DY are the components of the velocity in x and y directions. (x is the direction from left to right and y is the direction from top to bottom.)

Figure 11.15. Default Physics Definition for the ball

For now, let's set the Physics Definition of the ball as shown in Figure 11.16.

By these settings, the ball will be affected by gravity, will bounce off without losing its energy and will not have any damping. When you run the game in the simulator, you will see the ball falling off the screen ☺. It is because the scene edges do not have borders by default.

In order to make the ball bounce off the floor, we need to add Code 11.1 inside of the **didMove(to view: SKView)** class in the GameScene.swift file.

```
let borderBody = SKPhysicsBody(edgeLoopFrom: self.frame)
borderBody.friction = 0
self.physicsBody = borderBody
```
Code 11.1

This code creates a border at the edges of the self.frame (which is the whole screen), then sets its friction to 0 (hence the ball will not lose energy during the bounce offs), and finally applies this border node to the scene. After adding this code, our **didMove(to view: SKView)** class will look like Code 11.2 (note that I removed the unused default code):

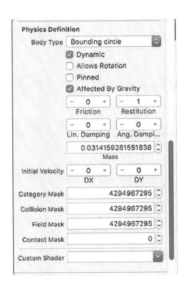

Figure 11.16. New Physics Definition for the ball

```
override func didMove(to view: SKView) {
        let borderBody = SKPhysicsBody(edgeLoopFrom:
self.frame)
        borderBody.friction = 0
        self.physicsBody = borderBody
    }
```
Code 11.2

Now, let's run our game in the simulator and we will see that the ball will fall and bounce off the floor infinitely (until we stop the simulator ☺). This is because we didn't set any damping on the ball and the Restitution is 1 meaning that the ball bounces off the floor without losing any energy. You can view the short clip of the game at this stage (Video 11.1) on the book's website: http://www.yamaclis.com/ios11.

You can play with the Physical Definition settings of the ball and run in the simulator to see how they affect its movement. For example if you set a linear damping as 0.2, the ball will lose its velocity continuously as it moves (Video 11.2 on the book's website).

Now, let's remove the effect of gravity from the ball so that we can clearly define the initial force on the ball. For this, select the ball to remove the gravity effect from its Physics Definition pane as in Figure 11.17.

If you run the game in the simulator now, you'll see that the ball stays at its initial place since there's no force acting on it initially. Let's apply an impulse (a sudden force) to the ball so that it starts moving in a direction we want. I applied a force of (dx: 10, dy= 20) by trial and error but you can apply any force you want as long as the ball strikes to all edges of the scene. The code for applying the impulse is given in Code 11.3.

```
let ball = childNode(withName: "ball") as! SKSpriteNode
ball.physicsBody!.applyImpulse(CGVector(dx: 10, dy: 20))
```
Code 11.3

In this code, a **SpriteKitNode** called **ball** is created to access the ball Sprite in the code. Then, the mentioned impulse is applied on the ball in the second line. Please add this code to **didMove(to view:  SKView)** and then if you run the game in the simulator, you'll see the ball striking the edges of the screen continuously (Video 11.3 on the book's website.).

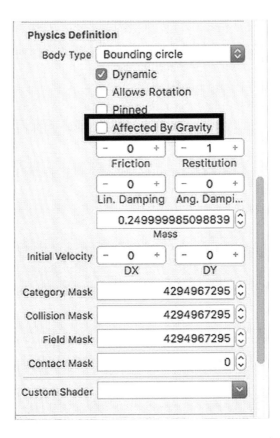

Figure 11.17. Removing the effect of the gravity from the ball

## 11.4. Adding the Shoe

It's now time to add the shoe that will prevent ball hitting the bottom of the scene and bounce the ball. Add a colour sprite close to the bottom edge and select the shoe as the texture as shown in Figure 11.18.

Now, set the size of the shoe as W=100 and L=50 and then the z position to 1. Remember that the z position of the background was 0 by default hence, by setting the z position of the shoe, we guarantee that the shoe will be shown on the background (z axis is from the screen towards the user). These settings are also shown in Figure 11.19 together with the added shoe in the scene.

| Sprite | |
|---|---|
| Name | shoe |
| Parent | Scene |
| ➡ Texture | shoe| |

Figure 11.18. Setting the newly added Sprite's properties

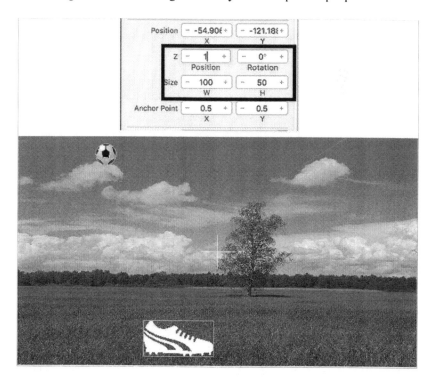

Figure 11.19. Setting the size and the z position of the shoe Sprite

We now need to define physics for the shoe since we want it to bounce the ball when the ball touches it. For this, choose the "Bounding rectangle" in the Physics Definition while the shoe Sprite is selected as shown below:

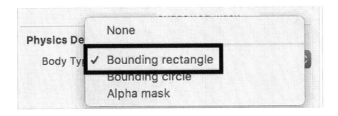

Figure 11.20. Choosing the "Bounding rectangle" for the shoe Sprite

In this pane, uncheck "Dynamic" and "Allows Rotation" checkboxes since we don't want the shoe to move when the ball hits it as shown in the following figure:

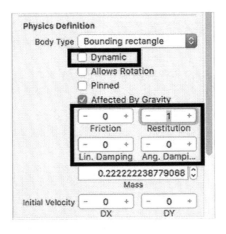

Figure 11.21. Physics Definition of the shoe

## 11.5. Moving the Shoe

We need to sense the touches on the shoe and move it according to these touches. First of all we need to define a variable to check the state of touching. Since there are only two possibilities: touching and not touching, it is OK to use a boolean variable. Please add this variable declaration before the class definition (just below the **import GameplayKit** line) in your GameScene.swift file:

```
var isGamerTouching = false
```
Code 11.4

The default value is **false** since the user will not be touching at the start of the game. In the default GameScene.swift file, there are readily placed lines regarding the touching. Delete all default code **after the** touchUp() function. Then, insert the following code in which functions for sensing the gamer touching and moving the shoe are implemented:

```
override func touchesBegan(_ touches: Set<UITouch>, with
event: UIEvent?) {
        let touch = touches.first
        let touchLocation = touch!.location(in: self)
        if let body = physicsWorld.body(at:
touchLocation) if body.node!.name == "shoe" {
                isGamerTouching = true
        }
    }
  }
override func touchesMoved(_ touches: Set<UITouch>, with
event: UIEvent?) {
 if isGamerTouching{
 let touch = touches.first
 let touchLocation = touch!.location(in: self)
 let previousLocation =
   touch!.previousLocation(in: self)
let shoe= childNode(withName: "shoe") as! SKSpriteNode
let shoeX = shoe.position.x + (touchLocation.x -
  previousLocation.x)
  shoe.position = CGPoint(x: shoeX, y: shoe.position.y)
        }
    }
    override func touchesEnded(_ touches: Set<UITouch>,
with event: UIEvent?) {
        isGamerTouching = false
    }

override func touchesCancelled(_ touches: Set<UITouch>,
with event: UIEvent?) {
        for t in touches { self.touchUp(atPoint:
t.location(in: self)) }
    }
    override func update(_ currentTime: TimeInterval) {

    }
```
Code 11.5

You can download the source files of the project from this book's website and also copy-paste these codes from there if you want.

In this code, **touchesBegan()** function checks if the shoe Sprite is touched. Then, **touchesMoved()** function moves the shoe by the position method applied on the shoe Sprite using the shoe's updated x coordinate **shoeX**. The **touchesEnded()** function just sets the **isGamerTouching** variable to false when the touching ends. Run the game in the simulator and you can move the shoe to bounce the ball. You can view its clip as Video 11.4 on the book's website. As you can see from this clip, the ball moves dizzyingly fast, you can decrease the initial impulse (see Code 11.3) to have a slower ball if you wish.

The ball bounces infinitely and nothing happens when the gamer misses the ball. The ball bounces off the ground and the game continues. We need a condition to end the game and give points when the user bounces the ball. There can be several ways to set game logic but the simplest is to end the game when the gamer misses the ball (= ball touches ground ) and the gamer increases his/her score by 1 when he/she bounces the ball with the shoe. Setting up this logic in the game code requires handling contacts of the Sprites.

## 11.6. Handling the Contacts and Finalizing Gameplay Settings

In order to handle contacts, we need to extend our main class with the class called **SKPhysicsContactDelegate** in the following way:

```
class GameScene: SKScene, SKPhysicsContactDelegate {
```
Code 11.6

In order to check which Sprites had a contact, we will use "categories". Each Sprite will be added to a different category. We have the ball, the shoe and the ground (bottom of the screen). We'll define the following category variables just below the **isGamerTouching** variable definition in the GameScene.swift file:

```
let BallCategory    : UInt32 = 0x1 << 0
let BottomCategory  : UInt32 = 0x1 << 1
let ShoeCategory    : UInt32 = 0x1 << 2
```
Code 11.7

In fact, these are just integers having the values of 1, 2 and 4. However, it is convenient to define the categories in the above manner to track the contacts if there are loads of touching Sprites. The << operator shifts the bits from right to left effectively multiplying the number by 2.

In the first line 0x1 is the byte 00000001, middle one is 00000010 and the last one being 00000100. These are called binary numbers. In binary numbers, each digit has the multiplier of the powers of 2 unlike the decimals which have the multipliers of the powers of 10 per digit. Anyway, don't worry if these don't mean a lot for you. Just keep in mind that 0x1 <<0 is 1, 0x1 <<1 is 2 and 0x1 << 2 is 4.

We'll keep the score of the gamer in an integer which will increment by 1 for each bounce. Thus we can define an integer variable for this aim. Moreover, we'll display this score on the game screen (right top for example) therefore we need a SpriteKit Label to show this info to the gamer. For these, we can add the following code lines just below the category variable definitions:

```
var scoreInt: Int = 0
var scoreLabel = SKLabelNode(fontNamed:"Arial")
```
Code 11.8

Then, add the following code to **didMove()** function in order to access the bottom and the shoe in the game code to check contacts:

```
let bottomRect = CGRect(x: frame.origin.x, y:
frame.origin.y, width: frame.size.width, height: 1)
let bottom = SKNode()
bottom.physicsBody = SKPhysicsBody(edgeLoopFrom:
bottomRect)
addChild(bottom)
let shoe = childNode(withName: "shoe") as! SKSpriteNode
```
Code 11.9

We will now assign bottom, ball and the shoe to the respective categories using the code shown below (please add this code also to the **didMove()** function):

```
bottom.physicsBody!.categoryBitMask = BottomCategory
ball.physicsBody!.categoryBitMask = BallCategory
shoe.physicsBody!.categoryBitMask = ShoeCategory
```
Code 11.10

We want the game engine to check if the ball contacts to the bottom edge or the shoe. If it contacts the bottom edge, the game will be over and if touches the shoe, gamer's score will increment. The following code, which should be placed just after the above code, initializes the contact tests:

```
ball.physicsBody!.contactTestBitMask = BottomCategory |
ShoeCategory
physicsWorld.contactDelegate = self
```
Code 11.11

Finally, please place the following code inside the **didMove()** function to set the position of the score label:

```
scoreLabel.text = "Score: " + String(scoreInt)
scoreLabel.fontSize = 25
scoreLabel.position = CGPoint(x:(self.frame.maxX)*0.8,
y:(self.frame.maxY)*0.8)
scoreLabel.zPosition = 2
self.addChild(scoreLabel)
```
Code 11.12

In the above code, the score label will be positioned at the 0.8 x (screen width) and 0.8 x (screen height) with a font size of 25. You can change this position if you wish.

Finally, let's write the contact handling code. The BallCategory, BottomCategory and ShoeCategory have the values of 1, 2 and 4, respectively (see Code 11.6). Hence if a contact happens and if the contacting Sprites have the categories of 1 and 4, the score will be incremented by one. However, if a contact happens and the categories of contacts are 1 and 2, it means that the ball contacted the bottom edge (the gamer missed the ball). In this case the game will be over. A "Game over." text will appear on the screen. It is also good to remove the ball from the scene. The following contact function is a delegate of the **SKPhysicsContactDelegate** class and this function is added inside the GameScene.swift file (just below all other codes existing in GameScene.swift):

```
func didBegin(_ contact: SKPhysicsContact) {
if contact.bodyA.categoryBitMask == 4 &&
contact.bodyB.categoryBitMask == 1 {

scoreInt = scoreInt + 1
print(scoreInt)
scoreLabel.text = "Score: " + String(scoreInt)
        }

if contact.bodyA.categoryBitMask == 2 &&
contact.bodyB.categoryBitMask == 1 {

let ball = childNode(withName: "ball") as! SKSpriteNode
ball.removeFromParent()
var myLabel:SKLabelNode!
myLabel = SKLabelNode(fontNamed: "Arial")
myLabel.text = "Game over."
myLabel.fontSize = 50
myLabel.fontColor = SKColor.red
myLabel.position = CGPoint(x: self.frame.midX, y:
self.frame.midY)
myLabel.zPosition = 4
self.addChild(myLabel)
        }
    }
```
Code 11.13

When the ball contacts the bottom, the ball is removed using the **removeFromParent()** method:

```
ball.removeFromParent()
```
Code 11.14

After the ball is removed, a big red annoying "Game over." text appears in the middle of the screen. You can download project files including the whole GameScene.swift file on the book's website if you wish. Moreover Video 11.5 on the book's website shows a short gameplay and game over scene of our Bounce the Ball game.

## 11.7. The Game

Screenshots during the gameplay and the game over scene are also shown in Figures 11.22 and 11.23 (colour figures and clips available at www.yamaclis.com/ios11):

Figure 11.22. Bounce the Ball game during gameplay

You can make the game more fun with simple tricks like increasing the initial velocity or controlling the shoe in a nonlinear way.

As you can see from this simple game, developing games is a serious job and requires hard work.

Figure 11.23. The game over scene

# EPILOGUE AND FUTURE WORK

I really hope that you enjoyed this book and got some confidence for developing iOS apps. If you would like to share your complaints and suggestions, please feel free to drop me an e-mail at syamacli@gmail.com or alternatively you can share it publicly on the comments section of the book's website www.yamaclis.com/ios11.

This book was intended to be a starter's guide. If you have followed this book thoroughly, you should be ready to learn more on iOS app development and the first source for this is, of course, the Internet. I recommend the following websites for advanced subjects:

- http://noeticforce.com/best-swift-tutorials-with-examples
- http://www.ioscreator.com/
- https://www.codeschool.com/learn/ios

I'd like to finish this book with the following quotes which I think have deep meanings:

*"We can only see a short distance ahead, but we can see plenty there that needs to be done."*

Alan Turing

*"Very little is needed to make a happy life; it is all within yourself, in your way of thinking."*

Marcus Aurelius

**Information is the resolution of uncertainty.**

E. Claude Shannon

———————— Keep calm and have a cup of tea. ☺ ————————

# REFERENCES

1. https://swift.org

2. https://developer.apple.com/

3. http://www.tiobe.com/tiobe-index/,

4. https://developer.apple.com/swift/resources/

5. Neil Smyth, iOS 10 App Development Essentials, eBookFrenzy, 2016.

6. http://www.learnswift.tips/

7. Christian Keur and Aaron Hillegaas, iOS Programming: The Big Nerd Ranch Guide, Big Nerd Ranch Guides, 2017.

8. John Ray, iOS 9 Application Development in 24 Hours, Sams Publishing, 2016.

9. Andrew Johansen, iOS 9: App Development - The Ultimate Beginner's Guide!, CreateSpace Independent Publishing Platform, 2016.

10. Matthew Mathias and John Gallagher, Swift Programming: The Big Nerd Ranch Guide, Big Nerd Ranch Guides, 2016.

11. http://www.kylejlarson.com/blog/iphone-6-screen-size-web-design-tips/

12. http://iosres.com/

**Password for the compressed files downloaded from the book's website http://www.yamaclis.com/ios11: 27A100**

70906832R00122

Made in the USA
San Bernardino, CA
08 March 2018